Charles Rackemann

**The land registration act of Massachusetts**

Which took effect October 1, 1898

Charles Rackemann

**The land registration act of Massachusetts**
*Which took effect October 1, 1898*

ISBN/EAN: 9783337257439

Printed in Europe, USA, Canada, Australia, Japan

Cover: Foto ©Andreas Hilbeck / pixelio.de

More available books at **www.hansebooks.com**

THE

# LAND REGISTRATION ACT

OF

# MASSACHUSETTS,

WHICH TOOK EFFECT OCTOBER 1, 1898.

WITH AN INTRODUCTORY STATEMENT, ANNOTATIONS,
CROSS REFERENCES, AND CITATIONS OF
CASES BEARING UPON IT.

BY

CHARLES S. RACKEMANN,

OF THE SUFFOLK BAR.

BOSTON:
LITTLE, BROWN, AND COMPANY.
1898.

𝔘niversity 𝔓ress:

JOHN WILSON AND SON, CAMBRIDGE, U.S.A.

# PREFACE.

THE TORRENS SYSTEM of Registration of Title to Land, as it was enacted by the Legislature of Massachusetts during the session of 1898, is presented to the profession and the public in the following pages.

The official text has been here reproduced, accompanied by full cross references, notes, and citations of authorities bearing upon the interpretation and construction of the act.

The field here entered by Massachusetts is, so far as the United States is concerned, almost *terra incognita*, for in only two of our States has any serious attempt been made to engraft this method upon our land law system; and in both those instances the validity of the action taken by the Legislature was questioned in the courts; and no sufficient practical test of the workings of such system in this country has yet become possible.

The editor has not felt it to be within his province at this time to enter upon any actual discussion or argument upon the merits or demerits of the present act, whether regarded as a piece of legislative enactment, or as a very serious innovation in a

practical way upon the laws and customs of conveyancing in Massachusetts.

But an effort has been made — so far as possible
within the limits of time and space — to present
this new law to owners of and dealers in land, and
their professional advisers, in such a way as to
enable them to understand it without loss of time,
and to perceive the advantages and disadvantages
of it, not overlooking the fact that it is open to
question and criticism.

In the Bibliography (which comes after the Act
in this volume) mention is made of the principal
discussions and treatises relating to the system
which have hitherto been published in the English language. It cannot be said that this is
complete, but it will serve as a guide to those
readers who may wish to go deeper into the
subject.

But for the very able assistance afforded by
William De Lancey Howe, Esq., of the Suffolk
Bar, and Mr. Francis Noyes Balch (now in the
Harvard Law School), this book could not have
been produced at this time; and the preparation
of the Index devolved almost wholly upon them.

CHARLES S. RACKEMANN.

Boston, October 1, 1898.

# TABLE OF CASES.

# INTRODUCTION.

THE Torrens System of Registration and Transfer of Title to real property, though a comparatively new subject in the United States, has been in operation in various parts of the United Kingdom since its adoption in 1856 by the colony of South Australia.

The system takes its name from Sir Robert Torrens, Bart., who was born in England in 1814, and who in 1841 was made, by the British Admiralty Office, an official in the Custom House at Adelaide. About the year 1850 he became interested in the Australian system of conveyance by deed and recording (which was substantially like that now generally in force throughout the United States), and was convinced that, because of its lack of simplicity, accuracy, expedition, and economy, it was out of harmony with the practical ideas and the progress of the age, and that the law on the tenure and transfer of land should create as much certainty on the one hand, and permit of as much despatch on the other, as were obtained through that branch of the law governing the transfer and registration of title to ships.

Although Torrens was not a member of the legal profession, he had mastered the principles

of admiralty law, and through his work in the
Custom House had become familiar with their
practical application.  Upon this foundation, and
with the perseverance and indomitable spirit of
a true reformer, he set himself the task of over-
throwing the ancient and venerated laws relating
to land tenure and transfer, and of establishing
in their stead an entirely new system.

He found that there had existed in Austria,
Germany, Prussia, and Hungary, for a century
or more, a custom of registering land titles, and
upon this system, and his own for registering
ships, he formulated and adapted to the spirit of
the times, and to the needs of the business world,
a system for the registration and transfer of title
to real property.

In 1856 the system went into operation in South
Australia with Torrens as Registrar-General, and
under his direction and superintendence it was
made a success, its chief advantages over the old
method being, first, the indefeasible nature of the
title secured under it, and secondly, through the
abrogation of the necessity of abstracts of title,
speed, certainty, and economy of transfer.  The
step thus taken by South Australia was soon followed by her sister colonies, — Victoria, New South
Wales, Queensland, Tasmania, and New Zealand,
— until finally entire Australasia adopted the
Torrens system.

As early as 1854, a Royal Commission was appointed in England to investigate the prevailing
systems of dealing in land, and to recommend
the adoption by England of a new system, which,

among other advantages over the old, would first of all lessen the time and cost expended between the making of a bargain for the sale of land and the completion of a sale, and, secondly, render it unnecessary that the same process of investigation in a title should be gone through with on every subsequent purchase or mortgage. Before the Commission made its report in 1857, however, Robert Torrens had published in England a pamphlet setting forth his ideas on the subject of land transfer, while in 1856 the system created by him had already been adopted in South Australia.

As a result of the report of the Royal Commission, there was passed in England, in 1862, "An Act to Facilitate the Proof of Title to and the Conveyance of Real Estate" (25–26 Vict. cap. 53), better known as "Lord Westbury's Act." While this Act was along the lines set forth in the Torrens system, it yet varied from it in so many important features that, as Torrens predicted, it failed of complete success, although during its short existence it was estimated that property to the value of £6,000,000 had been registered under it.

In 1868 Lord Cairns, then Lord Chancellor, obtained a Royal Commission to be appointed for the purpose of inquiring into the operation of Lord Westbury's Act, and reporting whether any alteration or amendment would better be made. The report of the Commission, published in 1870, condemned the system of registration of title established by the Act of 1862 on account of the necessity which it imposed of (1) showing a marketable title,

(2) defining boundaries, and (3) registering partial interests; yet recommended its continuance, and also the establishment of a new registry on the principles set forth in the report of 1857. The result of the recommendations of the Commission was the introduction in 1873 of a "Land Transfer Act" (38–39 Vict. cap. 87), which was passed in 1875, and which, known as the "Lord Cairns Act," is now in force in England. As yet only a comparatively small part of the landowners have availed themselves of the benefits of the Act, but the Registrar-General reports that the number of registered owners has been steadily increasing, and that the manifest advantages of a registered title are gradually overcoming the deep-rooted opposition of the English landowner to having his title a matter of public record.

In British Columbia a system for the registration of titles has been in operation since 1870, while in that section known as Vancouver Island, its principles were adopted as early as the year 1861. The Land Titles Act passed by the Province of Ontario in 1885, and the Real Property Act adopted in the Province of Manitoba in the same year, are both based upon the Imperial Act of 1875.

In the year 1892, the Commission appointed by the General Assembly of the State of Illinois to investigate the Torrens system of transferring land titles, submitted its report, and introduced "A Bill for an Act concerning Land Titles," which was the first legislative effort to adjust the Torrens system to the Constitution and the laws of this country. The closing section of that Act provided that it should not apply to land in any county until the Act had been adopted by a vote of the people of the county. The Act was passed by the Legislature, and approved by the Governor, June 13, 1895. At the fall elections that year, it was adopted by the people of Cook County (embracing Chicago) by a majority of 77,538; but in 1896, when the validity of the Act was tested in the case of The People v. Chase,[1] the Supreme Court of Illinois held it to be unconstitutional and void. In May, 1897, a second "Act concerning Land Titles" was passed, in which the Legislature attempted to avoid the objection to the former Act. This new Act was quickly carried before the Supreme Court of the State, in the case of The People v. Simon. The case was argued last spring, and has just been decided, the Court sustaining the constitutionality of the law.

The advocacy of the Torrens system at the World's Real Estate Congress, held at Chicago in October, 1893, resulted in the subject being taken up for consideration by the Bar Associations of the different States, and, we understand, in the appointment by the Legislatures of Maine, New York, Maryland, Ohio, and California of special commissions to study the system still further with a view to its adoption in those States.

In 1896 Ohio passed an Act embodying the principles of the system, but since the Act had followed closely the first Act in Illinois, and had become operative before the decision in the People v. Chase[1] was handed down, the Supreme Court of

---

[1] 165 Ill. 527.

Ohio, in the case of The State *v.* Guilbert,[1] held the
act to be unconstitutional and void.

In Massachusetts the principles of the Torrens
system have been under discussion for some years
past, and have been the subject of most careful
study and consideration.   How long the subject
has occupied the thoughts of its advocates here it
would, of course, be impossible to say; but as
early as January, 1891, the late Governor William
E. Russell, in his inaugural address, referred to the
necessity of a thorough reform in our methods of
land transfer and registration, and stated that the
Torrens system would be called to the attention
of the Legislature through a special message.   In
this message, which is dated February 17, 1891,[2]
he says : —

"I believe that the Australian system of land registration and transfer, more commonly referred to, from
the name of its originator, as the Torrens system, is the
longest step that has yet been taken anywhere towards
that freedom, security, and cheapness of land transfer
which is conceded to be so desirable in the interests of
the people.   Our citizens demand the enactment of the
best legislation that can be devised, whether originated
here or elsewhere, and while another country whose
conditions are similar to our own has gained the credit
of first adopting the admirable and simple plan of land
transfer which I now call to your attention, we can yet
be the first among the States of the Union to place
this legislation upon our statute book, and to lead the
way in its adoption by the American people, as we have
already done in the case of the Australian ballot.   The
universal favor with which this latter system has been

---

[1] 56 Ohio State, 575 (1897).
[2] Acts and Resolves of Massachusetts, 1891, p. 1143.

received by our people should at least remove any prejudice against following the legislation of the same country
in another respect."

After dwelling at length upon the merits of the
Torrens system, and likewise on the advantage
which would be reaped by the citizens of the Commonwealth through its adoption, the message is
closed by recommending the appointment of a
special commission, to be charged with the duty of
giving public hearings on the matter, and reporting to the next Legislature the draft of a proper
Act.

Accordingly, under Chapter 100 of the Acts
of 1893, the Legislature passed "An Act authoriz-
ing the Appointment of a Commission to draft
an Act embodying the Principles of the Torrens
System of Land Transfer." By virtue of this Act
a commission was appointed consisting of James
R. Carret and Heman W. Chaplin, Esquires, of
Boston, and Frederick H. Stebbins, Esquire, of
Springfield, who in March, 1894, laid before the
General Court a majority bill from Mr. Carret and
Mr. Stebbins, and a minority bill from Mr. Chaplin,
both bills, however, embodying substantially the
Torrens system of registration of title.

Under Chapter 511 of the Acts of 1897, authorizing the Governor to appoint a committee to draft
an Act embodying the principles of the Torrens
system of land transfer, the Governor appointed
as the sole member of this committee Alfred Hem-
enway, Esquire, of Boston, who on January 3, 1898,
submitted to the Legislature the draft for the "Act
to Provide for Registering and Confirming Titles

to Land," which, being duly passed, on receiving the Governor's approval on June 23, 1898, marked the adoption by Massachusetts of the Torrens system.

The principles of the system may be stated, briefly, as follows : —

1. Public examination of title.
2. Registration of the title.
3. Issuance of a certificate of title.
4. Re-registration of title on every subsequent transfer.
5. Notice on the certificate of any matter affecting the registered title.
6. Indemnity against loss out of an assurance fund.

Under the Torrens system as adapted by the present "Land Registration Act" to the needs of Massachusetts, the Commonwealth provides a Court of Registration consisting of two judges, a recorder, who is the clerk of the court, and one or more examiners of title in each county. Any person claiming to own a piece of land may apply to the recorder, or the assistant recorder, at the registry of deeds for the district in which the land or any portion thereof lies, for registration of his title, submitting his deeds, plans, and other evidences of title. The recorder then causes an examination to be made by the examiners of title, and after proper notice and proceedings to enable all persons who may appear to have any adverse interests to assert them, if the title appears to be good, and no adverse claim is made, the recorder registers the title in a registration book. This

entry is styled the original certificate of title, an
exact copy of which, called the duplicate certificate, is then given to the applicant. If, however,
adverse claims are made, action upon the application is suspended until the claims are disposed of
in the Court of Registration, or, in case of appeal,
by the decision of the Superior Court or the Supreme Judicial Court. Any recognized encumbrances or limitations, such as trusts, easements,
mortgages, etc., are briefly noted on the certificates.
The registered title is by law made indefeasible,
that is, the certificate is given the effect of a decree of court which cannot be questioned. The
law also establishes the principle of "no transfer
except upon the books," which means that no subsequent act or proceeding is allowed to affect the
title to land once registered, unless it is brought to
the attention of the recorder, or assistant recorder,
and a proper memorandum stating its effect is indorsed on the certificate. For example : the registered owner of land, desiring to mortgage it,
executes the customary mortgage deed, which,
with the owner's duplicate certificate, is presented
to the assistant recorder, who thereupon enters
upon the original certificate, and also upon the
owner's duplicate certificate, a memorandum of
the purport of the mortgage deed, together with
the time of filing and a reference to the registration book, and furthermore delivers to the mortgagee a duplicate of the certificate of title, like the
owner's duplicate, except that it bears upon its face
the words " Mortgagee's duplicate." When the
mortgage is discharged, as it may be by the mort-

gagee in person on the registration book in the same manner as a mortgage on unregistered land, by an entry on the record book, the mortgagee's duplicate certificate is surrendered and stamped "Cancelled." And in like manner, attachments and other liens or adverse claims are noted on the owner's duplicate certificate, the result being that under the Torrens system it is possible to ascertain with much greater certainty, quickness, and economy than heretofore, by a mere inspection of the certificate on record, the state of the title to any piece of land.

One other feature of the system deserves special notice. When land is first registered, or when it passes by will or descent, the applicant, devisee, or heir pays to the recorder one tenth of one per cent of the assessed value of the real estate. The sums so paid constitute an "Assurance Fund," which is held by the Treasurer of the Commonwealth to indemnify any person who, without negligence on his part, sustains loss or damage, or is deprived of land or of any estate or interest therein, by virtue of the registration of the title to such land.

The foregoing outline of the Massachusetts Torrens Act serves to give a general idea of its essential provisions, and at once invites critical examination of them in detail, and likewise a comparison of the new system with the existing order of things relating to the conveyance of land.

How far the system is an answer to the problem, arising as far back in our history as the time when our ancestors first settled on the shores of Massachusetts Bay, of providing a safe and practicable method "for avoyding all fraudulent conveyances, & that every man may know what estate or interest other men may have in any houses, lands, or other hereditaments they are to deal in" (Mass. Col. Rec., I. 306), now depends upon whether the public and their advisers in the profession of the law find it, after a fair and just trial, adequate to the needs of the Commonwealth.

THE

# LAND REGISTRATION ACT

OF

## MASSACHUSETTS.

PASSED BY THE LEGISLATURE IN 1898.

### [CHAP. 562.]

AN ACT TO PROVIDE FOR REGISTERING AND CON-
FIRMING TITLES TO LAND.

*Be it enacted, etc., as follows :*

SECTION 1. This act may be cited as the Land   Citation.
Registration Act.

#### COURT OF REGISTRATION.

SECTION 2. A court is hereby established, to   Court of Regis-
be called the Court of Registration, which shall   tration.
have exclusive original jurisdiction of all applications for the registration of title to land within
the Commonwealth, with power to hear and determine all questions arising upon such applications, and also shall have jurisdiction over such
other questions as may come before it under this
act, subject however to the right of appeal, as
hereinafter provided.[1]

The Illinois Act of 1895 made no provision for establishing a separate court of registration, but conferred judicial
powers upon the recorder of deeds, who by the Act was made

[1] See §§ 14, 16, 38.

registrar of titles.  The Supreme Court, in The People *v.* Chase, 165 Ill. 527 (1896), held this to be in violation of art. 6, § 1, of the constitution of Illinois, providing that the judicial powers should be vested in courts therein named.[1]

**Sittings.**

The court shall hold its sittings in Boston, but may adjourn from time to time to such other places as the public convenience may require.  In the county of Suffolk the board of aldermen of the city of Boston, and in other counties the county commissioners, shall provide suitable rooms for the sittings of the court of registration, in the same building with or convenient to the probate court or the registry of deeds, and shall provide all necessary books and such printed blanks and stationery for use in registration proceedings as may be ordered by the court.

**Jurisdiction.**

The court shall have jurisdiction throughout the Commonwealth, and shall always be open, except on Sundays and holidays established by law.  It shall be a court of record, and shall cause to be made a seal, and to be sealed therewith all orders, process, and papers made by or proceeding from the court and requiring a seal.  All notices, orders, and process of said court may run into any county and be returnable as the court may direct.

**Procedure.**

The court shall from time to time make general rules and forms for procedure, conforming as near as may be to the practice in the probate courts, but subject to the express provisions of this act and to general laws.  Such rules and forms before taking effect shall be approved by the supreme judicial court or a justice thereof.

[1] Cf. § 31 and note, and § 54.

In this act, except where the context requires "Court." a different construction, the word court shall mean the court of registration.

SECTION 3. The governor, with the advice and consent of the council, shall appoint two judges Two judges. of the court of registration, one of whom shall be appointed, commissioned and qualified as judge of registration, and the other as assistant judge of registration, each to hold his office during good behavior ; and any vacancy shall be filled in the manner provided by the constitution.

SECTION 4. The authority and jurisdiction of Authority and jurisdiction. the court of registration shall begin and take effect as soon as the judges thereof are appointed and qualified. The court may be held by a single judge, and when so held shall have all the authority and jurisdiction committed to said court. Different sessions may be held at the same time, Sessions. either in the same county or in different counties, as the judges may decide, and they shall so arrange the sessions as to insure a prompt discharge of the business of the court.

SECTION 5. Citations, orders of notice, and all Citations and orders. other process issuing from the court shall bear test of the judge of registration, and be under the seal of the court and signed by the clerk. Seal.

SECTION 6. In case of a vacancy in the office Vacancy, absence, etc. of judge of registration, or of his absence or inability to perform his duties, the assistant judge shall perform them, until the vacancy is filled or any disability is removed.

SECTION 7. The governor, with the advice and consent of the council, shall appoint a recorder, Recorder.

who shall be clerk of the court, and who shall hold his office for the term of five years. He shall attend the sessions of the court and keep a **Docket.** docket of all causes, and shall affix the seal of the court to all process or papers proceeding therefrom and requiring a seal.

SECTION 8. The recorder shall be under the **Custody of documents.** direction of the court, and shall have the custody and control of all papers and documents filed with him under the provisions of this act,[1] and shall carefully number and index the same. Said papers and documents shall be kept in Boston in an **Depository.** office to be called the Land Registration Office, which shall be near the court of registration. The recorder shall have authority, with the sanction of the court, to employ such assistants and messengers as may be necessary.

This provision seems at first sight to cause unnecessary expense and hardship for registration of land situated in counties distant from Boston. But, on the other hand, it will prove to be most convenient to have one central office at which facts as to registration or proposed registration in other districts can be learned.

**Recorder may act in any county.** SECTION 9. The recorder may act in any county, and after land has been registered under this act he may [2] make all memoranda affecting the title, and enter and issue certificates of title as provided herein.

**Registers of deeds to be assistant recorders.** SECTION 10. The registers of deeds in each registry district, after any land within their respective districts has been registered under this act, shall have the same authority as the recorder

---

[1] Cf. §§ 20, 57.          [2] Cf. § 20, note.

to make all memoranda affecting the title of such land, and to enter and issue new certificates of title as provided herein, and to affix the seal of the court to such certificates and duplicate certificates of title; but in executing the provisions of this act the registers of deeds shall be subject to the general direction of the recorder, in order to secure uniformity throughout the Commonwealth; and their official designation shall be assistant recorders for the registry district in which they are severally registers of deeds. In case of the death or disability of the recorder the assistant recorder for the Suffolk district shall perform the duties of the recorder until the vacancy is filled or the disability removed. *Vacancy in office of recorder.*

SECTION 11. The recorder and all assistant recorders shall be sworn before the judge of registration, and a record thereof shall be made. They shall give bond in a sum to be fixed by the court, for the faithful performance of their official duties, before entering upon the same. They may administer oaths in all cases in which an oath is required, to persons appearing before them in matters pertaining to the registration of land. They shall keep accurate accounts of all moneys received as fees or otherwise, which shall be subject to examination by the controller of county accounts, in the same manner as accounts of registers of deeds, and they shall pay over such moneys quarterly to the treasurer of the Commonwealth. In case of the absence of any assistant recorder the assistant register for the district, or if there is no assistant register the person act- *Qualification of officers. Powers. Accounts. Assistant Recorders.*

ing as clerk in the office of the register of deeds, shall perform the duties of the assistant recorder, and the assistant recorder shall be responsible for him.

**Examiners of title.** SECTION 12. The judge of registration may appoint one or more examiners of title in each county, who shall be attorneys at law, and shall be subject to removal by the supreme judicial court.

Questions will arise under this section as to the authority of an examiner appointed in one county to act in another, first, when the land lies in two or more counties; and second, when the whole chain of title is not to be found in one county. Rules framed by the court will probably solve the doubt.

**Salaries.** SECTION 13. The salary of the judge of registration shall be forty-five hundred dollars a year. The salary of the assistant judge of registration shall be four thousand dollars a year. The salaries of the recorder, assistant recorders, examiners of titles, and all assistants and messengers shall be fixed by the governor and council. All salaries **How paid.** and expenses of the court shall be paid from the treasury of the Commonwealth.

**Appeal to Superior and Supreme Courts.** SECTION 14. Every order, decision, and decree of the court of registration shall be subject to appeal to the superior court for the county where the land lies, concerning which the order, decision, or decree appealed from was made. The appeal shall be claimed and entered within thirty days from the date of such order, decision, or decree,[1] and the party appealing shall at the time

[1] See §§ 16, 63, ¶ 2.

of entering his appeal file in the superior court copies of all material papers in the case, certified by the recorder. Appearances and answers shall be filed in the superior court within thirty days *Answers.* after the appeal is entered,[1] unless for good cause further time is allowed, and upon the motion of either party the cause shall be advanced for speedy hearing, and shall be tried by the court, unless either party within the time allowed for entering appearance claims trial by jury, in which case issues for the jury shall be framed. Questions of law arising in the superior court may be taken to the supreme judicial court for revision by any party aggrieved, in the same manner as in proceedings at law in the superior court.

This provision seems to imply that lands lying in different counties or registry districts cannot be registered under one application, even though they constitute one estate or holding. Cf. §§ 20, 24, 29, and 41.

SECTION 15. At the end of the proceedings on *Final decree.* appeal the clerk of the superior court shall certify to the court of registration the final decision on the appeal, and the court of registration shall enter the final decree in the cause, in accordance with the certificate of the clerk of the superior court.

SECTION 16. If the party appealing does not *Appeal must be duly prosecuted.* duly prosecute his appeal within the time limited the original order, decision, or decree shall stand as if no appeal had been taken.[2]

SECTION 17. The court of registration in all *Court may enforce orders or decrees.* matters over which it has jurisdiction may enforce its orders or decrees, in the same manner as decrees

[1] See § 38.    [2] See §§ 14, 63, ¶ 2.

are enforced in equity, and upon the request of the judge of registration the sheriff of any county shall assign a deputy to attend the sittings of the court in that county.

Costs.

SECTION 18. Costs shall be taxed as in the superior court sitting in equity, where no different provision is made.

## ORIGINAL REGISTRATION.

Who may apply for Registration.

SECTION 19. Application for registration of title may be made by the following persons, namely :

Owner.

First. The person or persons claiming, singly or collectively, to own the legal estate in fee simple.

Appointor.

Second. The person or persons claiming, singly or collectively, to have the power of appointing or disposing of the legal estate in fee simple.[1]

Guardian.

Third. Infants and other persons under disability may make application by their legally appointed guardians; but the person in whose behalf the application is made shall be named as applicant.

Corporation.

Fourth. Corporations may make make application by any officer duly authorized by a vote of the directors : *provided, however,* that one or more

Tenants.

tenants for a term of years, which is regarded as a fee simple in section one of chapter one hundred and twenty-one of the Public Statutes,[1] shall not be allowed to make application except jointly

Reversioner.

with those claiming the reversionary interest which makes up the fee simple at common law ;

Mortgagor.

nor shall a mortgagor make application without

[1] Cf. § 48, and see § 104.

the consent in writing of the mortgagee; nor a married woman without the consent in writing of her husband, unless she holds the land as her separate property or has a power to appoint the same in fee simple, or has obtained a decree of the probate court under the provisions of chapter two hundred and fifty-five of the acts of the year eighteen hundred and eighty-five, as amended by chapter two hundred and ninety of the acts of the year eighteen hundred and eighty-seven;[1] nor one or more tenants claiming undivided shares less than a fee simple in the whole land described in the application.

<small>Married woman.</small>

<small>Tenants.</small>

Pub. Sts. ch. 121, § 1, provides, in substance, that where land is demised for the term of one hundred years or more, while fifty years thereof remain unexpired the term shall be regarded as an estate in fee simple.

Acts of 1885, ch. 255, as amended by Acts of 1887, ch. 290, provides, in substance, that a married woman may make a will as if sole, but cannot thereby, without her husband's written consent, deprive him of his tenancy by the curtesy, nor his right to use half her real estate for life, nor of more than half her personal property, unless she has a decree of court establishing the fact that she is deserted by her husband, or living apart from him for justifiable cause, in which case she may by will or deed without her husband's consent dispose of all her real and personal estate; or of her real estate not exceeding five thousand dollars, where no issue survives her.

SECTION 20. The application may be filed with the recorder, or with the assistant recorder at the registry of deeds for the district in which the land, or any portion thereof,[2] lies. Upon filing his

<small>Application to be filed.</small>

---

[1] Cf. § 14 and note.    [2] Cf. §§ 8, 41, 57.

application the applicant shall forthwith cause to be filed in the registry of deeds for the said district or districts a memorandum stating that application for registration has been filed, and the date and place of filing, and a copy of the description of the land contained in the application. This memorandum shall be recorded and indexed by the register with the records of deeds. Each assistant recorder shall also keep an index of all applications in his district, and in every case where the application is filed with him shall, after recording, transmit the same, with the papers and plans filed therewith, to the recorder.

*Memorandum.*

*Index.*

It seems that, where it is necessary to give effect to the clear intention of the Legislature, the word "may" is to be construed in a mandatory sense, but that where neither the context nor the general purpose of the act or instrument manifestly requires an unusual interpretation, its use is then merely directory. See Opinion of the Justices, 11 Pick. 543; Worcester Co. *v.* Schlesinger, 16 Gray, 168; Commonwealth *v.* Haynes, 107 Mass. 197; Hill *v.* Duncan, 110 Mass. 238; Commonwealth *v.* Smith, 111 Mass. 407; Phillips *v.* Fadden, 125 Mass. 198, 201.

*Application to be in writing.*

SECTION 21. The application shall be in writing, signed and sworn to by the applicant or by some person duly authorized[1] in his behalf. If there is more than one applicant the application shall be signed and sworn to by or in behalf of each. It shall contain a description of the land, and shall state whether the applicant is married; and if married the name of the wife or husband; and if unmarried whether he or she has been married,

*Contents.*

[1] "Duly authorized," see § 104. Letter of attorney, sealed, acknowledged, and recorded, is required.

and if so, when and how the marriage relation terminated; and if by divorce, when, where and by what court the divorce was granted.    It shall also state the name in full and the address of the applicant, and also the names and addresses of the adjoining owners and occupants, if known; and if not known it shall state what search has been made to find them.    It may [1] be in form as follows:

COMMONWEALTH OF MASSACHUSETTS.

*To the Honorable the Judge of the Court of Registration.*

I (or we) the undersigned, hereby apply to have the land hereinafter described brought under the operation and provisions of the land registration act, and to have my (or our) title therein registered and confirmed.    And I (or we) declare: (1) That I am (or we are) the owner (or owners) in fee simple of a certain parcel of land [2] with the buildings (if any, and if not, strike out the clause), situate in (here insert accurate description).    (2) That said land at the last assessment for taxation was assessed at        dollars; [3] and the buildings (if any) at        dollars.    (3) That I (or we) do not know of any mortgage or encumbrance affecting said land, or that any other person has any estate or interest therein, legal or equitable, in possession, remainder, reversion, or expectancy.    (If any, add "other than as follows," and set forth each clearly.)    (4) That I (or we) obtained title (if by deed, state name of grantor, date and place of record, and file the deed or state reason for not filing.    If in any other way, state it).    (5) That said land is        occupied.    (If occupied state name in full and place of residence and post office address of occupant and the nature of his occupancy.    If unoccupied, insert "not.")    (6) That the names in full and addresses as far as known to me (or us) of the occupants [4]

[1] See note to § 19.    The Court of Registration has adopted this form.

[2] All privileges and appurtenant easements should unquestionably be referred to at the end of the description of the land.

[3] The reason for this requirement is not apparent.    No provision is made for land which was assessed as part of a larger parcel.

[4] *Quære,* how far is this intended to apply to hotels, tenements, office buildings, apartment houses, etc. ?

of all lands adjoining said land are as follows: (Give street
and number wherever possible. If names not known state
whether inquiry has been made, and what inquiry.) (7) That
the names and addresses so far as known to me (or us) of the
owners of all lands adjoining the above land are as follows:
(Same directions as above.) (8) That I am (or we are) married. (Follow literally the directions given in section twenty-
one of the land registration act.) (9) That my (or our) full
name (or names), residence and post office address is (or are)
as follows:

Dated this        day of        in the year eighteen hundred
and ninety-

(Schedule of documents.)                    (Signature.)

COMMONWEALTH OF MASSACHUSETTS.

ss                                            189

Then personally appeared the above named        , known
to me to be the signer (or signers) of the foregoing application, and made oath that the statements made therein, so far
as made of his (or their) own knowledge are true, and so far
as made upon information and belief, that he (or they) believe
them to be true, before me,

*Justice of the Peace.*

**Non-resident applicant.**

SECTION 22. If the applicant is not a resident
of the Commonwealth he shall file with his application a paper appointing an agent residing in the
Commonwealth, giving his name in full and post
office address, and shall therein agree that the
service of any legal process in proceedings under
or growing out of the application shall be of the
same legal effect when made on said agent, as if
made on the applicant within the Commonwealth.
If the agent dies, or removes from the Commonwealth, the applicant shall at once make another
appointment; and if he fails to do so the court
may dismiss the application.

On foreign Executors and Trustees, see Pub. Sts. ch. 132,
§§ 8–13. On foreign Corporations, see Acts of 1884, ch. 330.

SECTION 23. Amendments to the application, including joinder, substitution, or discontinuing as to parties, shall be allowed by the court at any time upon terms that are just and reasonable; but all amendments shall be in writing, signed and sworn to, like the original.

Amendments.

Terms.

SECTION 24. An application may include two or more contiguous parcels of land within the same registry district.[1] But two or more persons claiming in the same parcels different interests, which collectively make up the legal estate in fee simple in each parcel, shall not join in one application for more than one parcel unless their interests are alike in each and every parcel. The court may at any time order an application to be amended by striking out one or more of the parcels, or by a severance of the application.

What application may include.

*Quære*, whether this refers to the quality or quantity of interests, or whether it includes both?

SECTION 25. If the application describes the land as bounded on a public or private way it shall state whether or not the applicant claims any and what land within the limits of the way, and whether the applicant desires to have the line of the way determined.

Land bounded on way.

SECTION 26. The applicant shall file with the application a plan[2] of the land, and all original muniments of title within his control mentioned in the schedule of documents. Such original muniments as affect land not included in the appli-

Plans.

Deeds.

[1] Cf. § 14.

[2] *Quære*, does this mean a plan drawn by an engineer after a survey of the land? See § 36.

cation may be withdrawn on filing certified copies
of the same. When an application is dismissed
or discontinued the applicant may, with the consent of the court, withdraw such original muniments of title.

**When subject to mortgage or lease.** SECTION 27. When an application is made
subject to an existing mortgage or lease, executed
by the applicant or some predecessor in title, the
applicant shall file with the application a certified
copy of the mortgage or lease, and cause the
original to be presented for registration, before
a decree of registration is entered.

Why the original in addition to the certified copy? The
mortgage or lease may be outside of the Commonwealth; and
even if inside the applicant has no power or authority to
compel its production. It may have been lost or destroyed.
What is to happen if it be not produced? See §§ 105 and
107.

**Court may require additional facts, etc.** SECTION 28. The court may by general rule
require facts to be stated in the application in
addition to those prescribed by this act, and not
inconsistent therewith, and may require the filing
of any additional papers.

**Proceedings not to bar sale, etc.** SECTION 29. After the filing of an application,
and before registration, the land therein described
may be dealt with, and instruments relating thereto
shall be recorded in the same manner as if no such
application had been filed; but all instruments left
for record relating to such land shall be indexed in
the usual manner in the registry indexes, and also
in the index of applications.[1] As soon as an application is disposed of the recorder shall make a

[1] Cf. § 39, sixth clause.

memorandum stating the disposition of the case, and shall send the same to the register of deeds for the proper district or districts,[1] who shall record and index it with the records of deeds, and in the index of applications. If the proceedings upon the application end in a decree of registration of title the land included therein shall, as soon as the said decree is transcribed, as hereinafter provided in section forty-one, become registered land, and thereafter no deeds or other instruments relating solely to such land shall be recorded with the records of deeds, but shall be registered in the registration book and filed and indexed with the records and documents relating to registered land.

Cf. § 41.

This provision is one of the most important and far reaching of all. In effect it requires one who sells or mortgages land, and also the vendee and mortgagee, to know whether or not the land has been previously registered by any former owner, and if he cannot satisfy himself on this point to deal with it at his peril. The provision points out emphatically the need of most thorough official indexes by localities as well as by names; and it may lead up to the introduction of the "Block system" as an integral part of efficacious land registration. See the pamphlet by John L. Thorndike, Esquire, published anonymously, and referred to in the Bibliography, p. 80. Cf. § 49.

Under the Victorian "Transfer of Land Statute," it has been held by the House of Lords that those dealing with land registered must ascertain at their own peril the existence and identity of the registered owner, the authority of his agent, and the validity of his deed, but need not investigate the title prior to such registration. Gibbs v. Messer, L. R. Appeal Cas. (1891), p. 248.

SECTION 30. Immediately after the filing of an application the court shall enter an order re-

[1] Cf. § 14.

Report of examiners. ferring it to one of the examiners of title, who shall search the records and investigate all facts stated in the application, or otherwise brought to his notice, and file in the case a report thereon, concluding with a certificate of his opinion upon the title. The recorder shall give notice to the applicant of the filing of such report. If the opinion of the examiner is adverse to the applicant he shall be allowed by the court a reasonable time in which to elect to proceed further or to withdraw his application. The election shall be made in writing and filed with the recorder.

Is the examiner to make his own search, or to confine his attention to information and matters supplied by the applicant? If the latter, the most interested party can produce or suppress what he thinks most helpful or adverse to his interests.

The examiner is given broader powers, and to a great extent control over interests in land, far beyond what auditors in cases at law, or masters in causes in equity, now have in Massachusetts. See note to § 2.

SECTION 31. If, in the opinion of the examiner, the applicant has a good title as alleged, and proper for registration, or, if the applicant after an adverse opinion of the examiner, elects to proceed further, the recorder shall, immediately upon the filing of the examiner's opinion, or the appli- Notice of application. cant's election, as the case may be, cause notice of the filing of the application to be published by the recorder in some newspaper published in the district where any portion of the lands lie. The notice shall be issued by the order of the court, attested by the recorder, and shall be in form substantially as follows:

### REGISTRATION OF TITLE.

SUFFOLK SS.                                COURT OF REGISTRATION.

To (here insert the names of all persons known to have an adverse interest, and the adjoining owners and occupants, so far as known), and to all whom it may concern:

WHEREAS an application has been presented to said court by (name or names and address in full) to register and confirm his (or their) title in the following described land (insert description).

You are hereby cited to appear at the court of registration to be held at        , in said county of        on the day of        , A. D.,        , at        o'clock in the forenoon, to show cause, if any you have, why the prayer of said application should not be granted. And unless you appear at said court at the time and place aforesaid your default will be recorded, and the said application will be taken as confessed, and you will be forever barred from contesting said application or any decree entered thereon.

WITNESS        Esquire, judge of said court, this day of        in the year eighteen hundred and ninety-

Attest:

*Recorder.*

Cf. § 5, which reads: "Citations, orders of notice, and all other process issuing from the *court* shall bear test of the judge of registration, and be under the seal of the *court* and signed by the clerk." It seems that the word "recorder" in the fifth line of the section must be a misprint for "court"; cf. § 92.

Is one publication enough?

Cf. § 5, requiring orders of notice, etc., to be "under the *seal* of the court."

Ought not the words "Commonwealth of Massachusetts" to appear also?

SECTION 32. The return day of said notice Return day. shall be not less than twenty nor more than sixty days from the date of issue. The court shall also, within seven days after publication of said notice Notices.

2

in a newspaper, cause a copy of the same to be mailed by the recorder to every person named therein whose address is known. The court shall also cause a duly attested copy of the notice to be posted in a conspicuous place on each parcel of land included in the application, by a sheriff or deputy sheriff, fourteen days at least before the return day thereof, and his return shall be conclusive proof of such service. If the applicant requests to have the line of a public way determined the court shall order notice to be given by the recorder, by mailing a registered letter to the mayor of the city or to one of the selectmen of the town or towns in which the land lies, or, if the way is a highway, to one of the county commissioners of the county or counties in which the land lies. If the land borders on a river, navigable stream, or shore, or on an arm of the sea where a river or harbor line has been established, or on a great pond, or if it otherwise appears from the application or the proceedings that the Commonwealth may have a claim adverse to that of the applicant, notice shall be given in the same manner to' the attorney-general. The court may also cause other or further notice of the application to be given in such manner and to such persons as it may deem proper. The certificate of the recorder that he has served the notice as directed by the court, by publishing or mailing, shall be filed in the case **Proof of service.** before the return day, and shall be conclusive proof [1] of such service.

---

[1] Conclusive proof, cf. § 109. Notice is a fact to be proved, like other facts, by evidence, either direct or circumstantial. See Am. and Eng.

SECTION 33. Upon the return day of the notice, and proof of service[1] of all orders of notice issued, the court may appoint a disinterested person to act as guardian *ad litem* for minors, and for all persons not in being who may have an interest. The compensation of the guardian or agent shall be determined by the court and paid as part of the expenses of the court.

*Guardian ad litem.*

SECTION 34. Any person claiming an interest, whether named in the notice or not, may appear and file an answer on or before the return day, or within such further time as may be allowed by the court. The answer shall state all objections to the application, and shall set forth the interest claimed by the party filing the same, and shall be signed and sworn to by him or by some person in his behalf.[2]

*Answer to application.*

SECTION 35. If no person appears and answers within the time allowed the court may at once upon motion of the applicant, no reason to the contrary appearing, order a general default to be

*Default.*

Encyc. of Law, 1st ed., vol. 16, p. 827. The weight of evidence is a matter exclusively for the jury. Ewing *v.* Burnet, 11 Pet. 41; Hyde *v.* Stone, 20 How. 170. And whether the evidence be sufficient is also a question for the jury. Metropolis Bank *v.* Guttschlick, 14 Pet. 19. A person not notified of an action nor a party thereto, and who had no right or opportunity to control the defence, to introduce or cross-examine witnesses, or to prosecute a writ of error, is not bound by the judgment therein rendered. Hale *v.* Finch, 104 U. S. 261. Suits at common law, within the meaning of the Seventh Amendment to the Constitution of the United States, giving the right of trial by jury, are all suits not of equity or admiralty jurisdiction in which legal rights are determined, whether by proceedings known to the common law or not. Parsons *v.* Bedford, 3 Pet. 433; see also Edwards *v.* Elliott, 21 Wall. 532; Pearson *v.* Yewdall, 95 U. S. 294; Walker *v.* Sauvinet, 92 U. S. 90.

[1] See note to previous section; also § 109.

[2] " In his behalf"; see § 21, note 1.

recorded and the application to be taken for confessed. By the description in the notice, " to all whom it may concern," [1] all the world are made parties defendant and shall be concluded by the default and order.[2] After such default and order the court may enter a decree confirming the title of the applicant and ordering registration of the same. The court shall not be bound by the report of the examiner of title, but may require other or further proof.

The Fourteenth Amendment of the Constitution of the United States provides that no State shall "deprive any person of life, liberty, or property without due process of law." In judicial proceedings "due process of law" requires notice, hearing, right of appeal, and final judgment. As to sufficiency of notice, the law seems to be that in proceedings *in personam* personal service, or its equivalent, by leaving a copy of the writ or summons at the defendant's last and usual place of abode, must be made ; while in proceedings *in rem*, when the process of the court issues against the thing which is in the custody of the court, and is technically the defendant, it is not essential to the jurisdiction that the persons having an interest in the thing to be affected by the judgment should have personal notice of the proceedings, or in fact any other notice than such as is implied by the seizure of the thing itself, and that consequently substituted service or notice by publication is sufficient. Pennoyer *v.* Neff, 95 U. S. 714 ; Freeman *v.* Alderson, 119 U. S. 185; Arndt *v.* Griggs, 134 U. S. 316 : The People *v.* Chase, 165 Ill. 527 ; State *v.* Guilbert, 56 Ohio St. 575.

See also D'Arcy *v.* Ketchum, 11 How. 165 ; Webster *v.* Reid, 11 How. 437 ; Cooper *v.* Reynolds, 10 Wall. 308 ; Eliot *v.* McCormick, 144 Mass. 10 ; Stone *v.* Wainwright, 147 Mass. 201 ; Needham *v.* Thayer, 147 Mass. 536 ; Rand *v.*

---

[1] See § 32, note, and §§ 38 and 92.
[2] Except as hereinafter provided ; see § 38.

Hanson, 154 Mass. 87; Short v. Caldwell, 155 Mass. 57; Mooney v. Hinds, 160 Mass. 469; Merrill v. Beckwith, 163 Mass. 503; Chase v. Henry, 166 Mass. 577; Kimball v. Sweet, 168 Mass. 105; Bordwell v. Collins, 44 Minn. 97; Brown v. Board of Levee Com., 50 Minn. 468.

It may be conceded, in the language of the United States Supreme Court, that "the power of the State to regulate the tenure of real property within her limits, and the modes of its acquisition and transfer, . . . is undoubted." United States v. Fox, 94 U. S. 315, 320; McCormick v. Sullivant, 10 Wheat. 202.

But such regulations must be exercised strictly in accordance with the provisions and limitations of the Constitution of the United States, and of the Constitution of the particular State the legislature of which exercises the power. Const. U. S. Amdt. XIV., and Mass. Dec. Rights, Art. XII.

The latest and most complete discussion of these principles is to be found in the case of Arndt v. Griggs, *supra.* See also United States v. Southern Pac. R. R., 63 Fed. Rep. 481.

The most striking point in the act under discussion is the fact that the proceedings are in substance instituted *ex parte* by an owner who desires to register land, and do not purport to be a trial of title, or a suit to remove clouds from title.

It is further to be observed that, in proceedings instituted under local statutes for quieting titles, it is essential to allege and prove the existence of some actual or possible claim of right or title adverse to that of the petitioner, or which, if valid, renders his ownership less than an absolute and entire fee simple. Such proceedings are efficient only in respect of such claim, and no pretence is made that they quiet the whole title of the petitioner as against all the world, or that they "bind the land" in respect of anything beyond the claim referred to in the petition. See Loring v. Hildreth, *in equity,* 170 Mass. 328.

Such proceedings differ in theory and in principle from cases where all the world are concluded in respect of the general title, as, for example, in cases of sale for non-payment of State, county, or municipal taxes, or for non-payment of United States revenue taxes, and the like.

There the sovereign power of the State, or that of the Federal government, is invoked because the public needs demand its exercise.

Such power never has been and apparently cannot be, under our existing constitutional protection, exercised in favor of an owner of land against claimants of rights or interests in the same property which he alleges are only derogatory of his control over the same, or stand between him and absolute ownership.

See note to § 85, *post*. And compare Article on Land Transfer Reform. — HARV. LAW REV., IV. p. 280.

In Hart *v.* Sansom, 110 U. S. 151, it was held that a decree of a State court for the removal of a cloud upon the title of land within the State, rendered against a citizen of another State, who has been cited by publication only, as directed by the local statutes, is no bar to an action by him in the Circuit Court of the United States to recover the land against the plaintiff in the former suit.

But this case was criticised and explained by later decisions of the United States Supreme Court, and declared upon re-examination not to be inconsistent with the earlier decisions of that court with which it was apparently in conflict.

The expression "due process of law" will be found further discussed in the following named cases, some of which, however, relate to criminal proceedings : Holland *v.* Challen, 110 U. S. 15; Boswell's Lessee *v.* Otis, 9 How. 336, 349 ; Parker *v.* Overman, 18 How. 137, 140 ; Clark *v.* Smith, 13 Pet. 195, 203 ; Pennoyer *v.* Neff, 95 U. S. 714, 727, 734 ; Huling *v.* Kaw Valley Ry., 130 U. S. 559, 563 ; Mellen *v.* Moline Iron Works, 131 U. S. 352 ; Leeper *v.* Texas, 139 U. S. 462 ; Caldwell *v.* Texas, 137 U. S. 692. See also 18 Stat. 472.

The question still remains whether the statement in the Act that the decree of registration "shall bind the land" leaves the case in the category of proceedings *in rem*, or in that of proceedings *in personam*.

If the proceedings for bringing land under the act can be said to be proceedings *in rem*, at common law, then these provisions for notice are apparently valid and sound, and the act is in respect of them constitutional.

If, on the other hand, they are proceedings *in personam*, these provisions are apparently unconstitutional.

That they fall in the latter category appears to be plain from the fact that the court created by the law is essentially made a court of equity by the very terms of the act.

See Loring *v.* Hildreth, *supra.*

SECTION 36. If in any case an appearance is entered and answer filed the cause shall be set down for hearing on the motion of either party, but a default and order shall first be entered against all persons who do not appear and answer, in the manner provided in the preceding section. The court may refer the cause or any part thereof to one of the examiners of title, as master, to hear the parties and their evidence, and make report thereof to the court. His report shall have the same weight as that of a master appointed by the superior court in equity, and he shall proceed according to the rules of said court applicable to masters,[1] except as the same may be modified by the rules of the court of registration. The court may in any case before decree require a survey to be made for the purpose of determining boundaries, and may order durable bounds to be set, and referred to in the application, by amendment. The expense of survey and bounds shall be taxed in the costs of the case, and may be apportioned among the parties as justice may require. If no persons appear to oppose the application, such expense shall be borne by the applicant.[2]

SECTION 37. If in any case the court finds that the applicant has not title proper for registration, a decree shall be entered dismissing the application, and such decree may be ordered to be without

*Hearing before examiner.*

*Surveys.*

*Expense.*

*Rejection or withdrawal of application.*

---

[1] See Rules of the Superior Court, XVIII., XXIII., XXX., XXXI., XXXII.

[2] See also § 26.

prejudice.[1]   The applicant may withdraw his application at any time before final decree, upon terms to be fixed by the court.

An interesting discussion of the effect of a withdrawal without prejudice by the defendant in an action is to be found in the case of Creighton *v.* Kerr, 20 Wall. p. 8.  Such withdrawal leaves the plaintiff with all advantages obtained during the proceedings up to that time.  But it may be open to question whether a dismissal by the court, in which the defendant or respondent takes no part, has the same effect.

**Decree of registration conclusive.**

SECTION 38.  If the court after hearing finds that the applicant has title as stated in his application, and proper for registration, a decree of confirmation and registration shall be entered. Every decree of registration shall bind the land,[2] and quiet the title thereto, subject only to the exceptions stated in the following section.  It shall be conclusive upon and against all persons, including the Commonwealth, whether mentioned by name in the application, notice or citation, or included in the general description " to all whom it may concern." [3]   Such decree shall not be opened by reason of the absence, infancy or other disability of any person affected thereby, nor by any proceeding at law or in equity for reversing judgments or decrees; subject, however, to the right of any person deprived of land or of any estate or interest therein by a decree of registration obtained by

**Final, except on review.**

fraud [4] to file a petition for review within one year after the entry of the decree, provided no innocent

---

[1] This matter is evidently left to the discretion of the court.

[2] See § 45.                    [3] See § 32, note, and § 35.

[4] See § 55.

purchaser for value has acquired an interest.[1]  If there is any such purchaser the decree of registration shall not be opened, but shall remain in full force and effect forever, subject only to the right of appeal hereinbefore provided.[2]  But any person aggrieved by such decree in any case may pursue his remedy by action of tort against the applicant or any other person for fraud in procuring the decree.[3]

For a discussion of the effect here attempted to be given to the decree of registration, see note to section 35, *supra*.

SECTION 39.  Every applicant receiving a certificate of title in pursuance of a decree of registration, and every subsequent purchaser of registered land who takes a certificate of title for value and in good faith, shall hold the same free from all encumbrances except those noted on the certificate, and any of the following encumbrances which may be subsisting, namely : — *Encumbrances.*

First.  Liens, claims or rights arising or existing under the laws or constitution of the United States which the statutes of this Commonwealth cannot require to appear of record in the registry. *Liens.*

Second.  Taxes within two years after the same have been committed to the collector. *Taxes.*

Third.  Any highway, town way, or any private way laid out under the provisions of section sixty-five of chapter forty-nine of the Public Stat- *Under Pub. Sts.ch. 49, § 65.*

[1] Cf. § 14.  Except in cases of fraud there is no appeal after the expiration of thirty days from the entering of decree.
[2] See § 14.
[3] Quære as to case where decree may have been wrongfully or mistakenly, but not fraudulently procured?  See §§ 55, 96, 97.

utes,[1] or any act in amendment thereof or in substitution therefor, where the certificate of title does not state that the boundary of such way has been determined.

**Lease.**    Fourth. Any lease for a term not exceeding seven years.

**Assessment.**    Fifth. Any liability to assessment for betterments, or other statutory liability which may attach to land in this Commonwealth as a lien prior to, or independent of, the recording or registering of any paper: *provided, however*, that if **Easements.** there are easements or other rights appurtenant to a parcel of registered land which for any reason have failed to be registered,[2] such easements or rights shall remain so appurtenant notwithstanding such failure, and shall be held to pass with the land until cut off or extinguished by the registration of the servient estate, or in any other manner.

**Conveyances.**    Sixth. Any conveyances, liens or other encumbrances made subsequent to the filing of the application for original registration and prior to the transcription of the decree for registration by the assistant recorder.[3]

This provision seems most unsatisfactory and too far-reaching. It puts it in the power of the applicant to nullify all the proceedings without any withdrawal or other action on his part in the suit in the court of registration, by the simple making and delivery of a deed. Cf. also § 59.

[1] Ch. 49, § 65, provides that "The selectmen or road commissioners may lay out or alter town ways for the use of their respective towns, and private ways for the use of one or more of the inhabitants thereof; or may order specific repairs to be made upon such ways."

[2] See § 21, note 2.            [3] Cf. § 29.

Seventh. Any attachments on mesne process. Attachment.

Section 40. Every decree of registration shall Decree of registration.
bear date of the year, day, hour and minute of
its entry, and shall be signed by the recorder. It
shall state whether the owner is married or unmarried, and if married the name of the husband
or wife. If the owner is under disability it shall
state the nature of the disability, and if a minor
shall state his age. It shall contain a description
of the land as finally determined by the court,
and shall set forth the estate of the owner, and
also, in such manner as to show their relative
priority, all particular estates, mortgages, easements, liens, attachments and other encumbrances,
including rights of husband or wife, if any, to
which the land or the owner's estate is subject,
and may contain any other matter properly to be
determined in pursuance of this act. The decree shall be stated in a convenient form for transcription upon the certificates of title hereinafter
mentioned.

Section 41. Immediately upon the entry of Decree to be recorded.
the decree of registration the recorder shall send
a certified copy thereof, under the seal of the
court, to the register of deeds for the district or
districts in which the lands lie, and the register
as assistant recorder shall transcribe the decree
in a book to be called the registration book, in
which a leaf or leaves in consecutive order shall
be devoted exclusively to each title.[1] The entry

---

[1] What is to happen when two registered parcels are united in one
ownership? Are they to go on as two titles, or to be consolidated?
Cf. § 44.

made by the assistant recorder in this book in
each case shall be the original certificate of title,
and shall be signed by him and sealed with the seal
of the court. All certificates of title shall be numbered consecutively, beginning with number one.
The assistant recorder shall in each case make an

*Owner's dupli-
cate certificate.* exact duplicate of the original certificate, including the seal, but putting on it the words, " Owner's
duplicate certificate," and deliver the same to the
owner, or to his attorney duly authorized.[1] In
case of a variance between the owner's duplicate
certificate and the original certificate the original
shall prevail. The certified copy of the decree of
registration shall be filed and numbered by the
assistant recorder, with a reference noted on it
to the place of record of the original certificate of
title: *provided, however,* that when an application
includes land lying in more than one district the
court shall cause the part lying in each district
to be described separately by metes and bounds
in the decree of registration, and the recorder shall
send to the assistant recorder for each registry
district a copy of the decree containing a description of the land within that district, and the assistant recorder shall register the same and issue
an owner's duplicate therefor, and thereafter for
all matters pertaining to registration under this
act the portion in each district shall be treated as
a separate parcel of land.[2]

SECTION 42. The certificate first registered in
pursuance of a decree of registration in regard to
any parcel of land shall be entitled in the regis-

---

[1] See § 21, note.          [2] See § 14.

tration book, " Original certificate of title, en- Original certificate.
tered pursuant to decree of the court of regis-
tration, dated at" (stating time and place of
entry of decree and the number of the case).
The certificate shall take effect from the date
of the transcription of the decree. Subsequent
certificates relating to the same land shall be in
like form, but shall be entitled " Transfer from Transfer.
No. " (the number of the next previous certificate relating to the same land), and also the words,
" Originally registered " (date, volume and page of
registration).

SECTION 43. Where two or more persons are Tenants in common.
registered owners as tenants in common, or otherwise, one owner's duplicate certificate may be
issued for the whole land, or a separate duplicate may be issued to each for his undivided
share.

SECTION 44. A registered owner holding one Separate certificates.
duplicate certificate for several distinct parcels of
land may surrender it, with the approval of the
court, and take out several certificates for portions
thereof. So a registered owner holding separate
duplicate certificates for several distinct parcels
may surrender them, and, with like approval,
take out a single duplicate certificate for the
whole land, or several certificates for different
portions thereof. Any owner subdividing a tract Plan of subdivision.
of registered land into lots shall file with the
recorder a plan of such land, when applying for
a new certificate or certificates, and the court
before issuing the same shall cause the plan to
be verified, and require that all boundaries, streets

and passageways shall be distinctly and accurately delineated thereon.[1]

**Registration runs with the land.** SECTION 45. The obtaining of a decree of registration and the entry of a certificate of title shall be regarded as an agreement running with the land,[2] and binding upon the applicant and all his successors in title that the land shall be and forever remain registered land, and subject to the provisions of this act and of all acts in amendment hereof.

**No title by prescription or adverse possession.** SECTION 46. No title to registered land in derogation of that of the registered owner shall be acquired by prescription or adverse possession.[3]

**Certificates conclusive evidence.** SECTION 47. The original certificate in the registration book, any copy thereof duly certified under the signature of the recorder or an assistant recorder, and the seal of the court, and also the owner's duplicate certificate, shall be received as evidence in all the courts of the Commonwealth, and shall be conclusive as to all matters contained therein, except so far as otherwise provided in this act.[4]

**Title.** SECTION 48. Every certificate of title shall set forth the names of all the persons whose estates make up the estate in fee simple in the whole land,[5] and duplicate certificates may be issued to each person, but the recorder or assistant recorder shall note in the registration book and on each duplicate, to whom such duplicate was issued.

[1] Cf. § 58.            [2] See § 38.

[3] Similar provisions exist in the English Act, 38 & 39 Vict. ch. 87, § 21, and in the Land Titles Act, 1885, § 25, of the Province of Ontario. This provision works a change in the law of Massachusetts. See Pub. Sts. ch. 126. Cf. the existing law as to non-acquirement of easements, Pub. Sts. ch. 122. And see § 70.

[4] See § 32, and note.            [5] Cf. § 19.

SECTION 49. The recorder, under the direction Indexes. of the court, shall make and keep indexes of all applications and of all decrees of registration, and shall also index and classify all papers and instruments filed in his office relating to applications and to registered titles. The recorder shall also, under the direction of the court, cause forms of Forms, etc. indexes and registration and entry books to be prepared for the use of the assistant recorders. The court shall prepare and adopt convenient forms of certificates of title, and shall also adopt general forms of memoranda to be used by the assistant recorders in registering the common forms of conveyance, and other instruments to express briefly their effect.[1]

## VOLUNTARY DEALING WITH LAND AFTER ORIGINAL REGISTRATION.

SECTION 50. An owner of registered land may Registered convey, mortgage, lease, charge or otherwise deal convey, etc. with the same as fully as if it had not been registered. He may use forms of deeds, mortgages, leases or other voluntary instruments like those now in use and sufficient in law for the purpose intended. But no deed, mortgage or other voluntary instrument, except a will and a lease for a term not exceeding seven years, purporting to convey or affect registered land, shall take effect as a conveyance or bind the land, but shall operate only as a contract between the parties, and as Contract. evidence of authority to the recorder or assistant

---

[1] Cf. § 29. And see the next section. See also § 79, directing that in cértain cases the certificate shall contain reference to matters or facts upon which the decree for registration is based.

Registration
necessary.

recorder to make registration.[1]  The act of registration shall be the operative act to convey or affect the land, and in all cases under this act the registration shall be made in the office of the assistant recorder for the district or districts where the land lies.

This section is one of the most important in the act. If registration by the recorder is alone sufficient to make the title perfect in the purchaser, then the recorder is the sole judge of the soundness and validity of the transfer, and if he misjudges or makes a mistake serious trouble will follow. On the other hand, if such registration is not sufficient, then the purchaser, by his counsel, as under our present system, must examine into and be satisfied of the validity and effect of the transfer. And in the latter case the alleged advantages of the new system would appear to have been exaggerated. And in either event, if the recorder is to register transfers and make memoranda based thereon, in his own sole discretion, is not the principle laid down in Illinois violated? And can such a provision as is made by this section be upheld? See note to § 1, *ante.* And even if this section is valid the practical working of it will not be clear until its provisions are supplemented by rules laid down by the Court of Registration.

Suppose that X. takes an absolute deed of registered land to the assistant recorder, without producing the owner's certificate or informing the recorder that the land is registered, and suppose further that X. does this in good faith. Is the assistant recorder to receive such deed in his character of assistant recorder, or in his capacity as register of deeds? Is he supposed to know that the land is registered land, or is he to ask X., and rely on his answer, or is he to inquire into it? Is X. to wait while he does so? If he is not to wait, what is to be the effect of his leaving the deed and marching off? These and further questions instantly suggest themselves, but the answers to them are not found in the act.

See again Gibbs v. Messer, already cited on page 15.

[1] See § 60. See § 52, which implies that the owner's duplicate certificate must be produced.

SECTION 51. Every conveyance, lien, attach-ment, order, decree, instrument or entry affecting registered land, which would under existing laws, if recorded, filed or entered in the registry of deeds, affect the real estate to which it relates, shall, if registered, filed or entered in the office of the assistant recorder of the district where the real estate to which such instrument relates lies, be notice to all persons from the time of such reg-istering, filing or entering. *Registration to be notice.*

The provisions of this section will strike the reader as in the nature of an apology for those of § 50. If registration alone works a conveyance or binds the land, what need of notice of anything after one registration until another is asked for ? And if purchasers are entitled to rely on reg-istration, what need of notice at all ? See note to § 50.

SECTION 52. No new certificate shall be entered or issued upon any transfer of registered land which does not divest the title in fee simple from the owner or some one of the registered owners. All interests in registered land less than an es-tate in fee simple shall be registered by filing with an assistant recorder the instrument creating or transferring or claiming such interest, and by a brief memorandum thereof made by an assistant recorder upon the certificate of title, and signed by him. A similar memorandum shall also be made on the owner's duplicate. The cancellation or extinguishment of such interests shall be regis-tered in the same manner.[1] *No new certifi-cate issued.*

SECTION 53. Where the assistant recorder is in doubt upon any question, or where any party in

[1] See § 50, and note.

interest does not agree as to the proper memorandum to be made in pursuance of any deed, mortgage or other voluntary instrument presented for registration, the question shall be referred to the court for decision, either on the certificate of the assistant recorder stating the question upon which he is in doubt, or upon the suggestion in writing of any party in interest; and the court, after notice to all parties and a hearing, shall enter an order prescribing the form of memorandum to the assistant recorder, who shall make registration in accordance therewith. .

*Question referred to court.*

Suppose that neither the parties nor the assistant recorder feels any doubt, but the latter acts under a mistake, what is the effect? See § 50, and note.

*Personal description in deeds.*

SECTION 54. Every deed or other voluntary instrument presented for registration shall contain or have indorsed upon it the full name, place of residence, and post office address of the grantee or other person acquiring or claiming an interest under such instrument, and every deed shall also state whether the grantee is married or unmarried, and if married, give the name in full of the husband or wife. Any change in the residence or post office address of such person shall be indorsed by an assistant recorder on the original instrument, on receiving a sworn statement[1] of such change. All names and addresses shall also be entered on all certificates. Notices[2] and process issued in relation to registered land in pursuance of this act may be served upon any person in interest by mailing the same to the

[1] Sworn to by whom?          [2] See § 5.

address so given, and shall be binding, whether such person resides within or without the Commonwealth.

Section 55. No new certificate of title shall be entered, and no memorandum shall be made upon any certificate of title by the recorder or any assistant recorder, in pursuance of any deed or other voluntary instrument, unless the owner's duplicate certificate is presented with such instrument, except in cases expressly provided for in this act or upon the order of the court, for cause shown, and whenever such order is made a memorandum thereof shall be entered on the new certificate of title and on the owner's duplicate. The production of the owner's duplicate certificate whenever any voluntary instrument is presented for registration shall be conclusive authority from the registered owner to the recorder or any assistant recorder to enter a new certificate or to make a memorandum of registration in accordance with such instrument, and the new certificate or memorandum shall be binding upon the registered owner and upon all persons claiming under him, in favor of every purchaser for value and in good faith : *provided, however*, that in all cases of registration procured by fraud the owner may pursue all his legal and equitable remedies against the parties to such fraud,[1] without prejudice, however, to the rights of any innocent holder for value of a certificate of title ; and *provided, further*, that after the transcription of the decree of registration on the original application, any subsequent registration under

*Certificate to be presented.*

*Fraud.*

[1] See §§ 38, 96, 97.

this act procured by the presentation of a forged duplicate certificate, or of a forged deed or other instrument, shall be null and void. In case of the

Loss. loss or theft of an owner's duplicate certificate notice shall be sent by the owner or by some one in his behalf to the assistant recorder for the district in which the land lies, as soon as the loss or theft is discovered.

Entry book. SECTION 56. Each assistant recorder shall keep an entry book in which he shall enter in the order of their reception all deeds and other voluntary instruments, and all copies of writs or other process filed with him relating to registered land. He shall note in such book the year, month, day, hour and minute of reception of all instruments, in the order in which they are received. They shall be

Time. regarded as registered from the time so noted,[1] and the memorandum of each instrument when made on the certificate of title to which it refers shall bear the same date.

Every deed or other instrument, whether voluntary or involuntary, so filed with the recorder or assistant recorder, shall be numbered and indexed, and indorsed with a reference to the proper certificate of title. All records and papers relating to registered land in the office of the recorder or of any assistant recorder shall be open to the public in the same manner as probate records are now open, subject to such reasonable regulations as the recorder, under the direction of the court, may make.

Duplicates of all deeds and voluntary instruments filed and registered may be presented with

---

[1] Cf. Pub. Sts. ch. 24. See also § 57.

the originals, and shall be attested and sealed by
the recorder or an assistant recorder, and indorsed
with the file number and other memoranda on the
originals, and may be taken away by the person
presenting the same.

Certified copies of all instruments filed and reg- Certified
istered may also be obtained at any time, on pay- copies.
ment of the assistant recorder's fees.

### CONVEYANCE IN FEE.

SECTION 57. An owner desiring to convey in
fee his registered land or any portion thereof shall
execute a deed of conveyance, which the grantor Deeds.
or the grantee may present to the assistant recorder
in the district where the land lies.[1] The grantor's
duplicate certificate shall be produced and presented
at the same time. The assistant recorder shall thereupon make out in the registration book a new cer- New certifi-
tificate of title to the grantee, and shall prepare cate.
and deliver to him an owner's duplicate certificate.
The assistant recorder shall note upon the original
and duplicate certificates the date of transfer, the
volume and page of the registration book where
the new certificate is registered, and a reference by
number to the last prior certificate. The grantor's
duplicate certificate shall be surrendered, and the
word "cancelled" stamped upon it. The original Cancellation.
certificate shall also be stamped "cancelled." The
deed of conveyance shall be filed,[2] and indorsed
with the number and place of registration of the
certificate of title of the land conveyed.

[1] See § 41, *proviso*.     [2] See §§ 8, 20, 56.

Deed for part of land.

SECTION 58. When a deed in fee is for a part only of the land described in a certificate of title, the assistant recorder shall also enter a new certificate and issue an owner's duplicate to the grantor for the part of the land not included in the deed. In every case of transfer the new certificate or certificates shall include all the land described in the original and surrendered certificates : *provided, however*, that no new certificate to a grantee of a part only of the land shall be invalid by reason of the failure of the assistant recorder to enter a new certificate to the grantor for the remaining unconveyed portion.[1]

Encumbrances.

SECTION 59. If at the time of any transfer there appears upon the registration book encumbrances or claims adverse to the title of the registered owner they shall be stated in the new certificate or certificates, except so far as they may be simultaneously released or discharged.[2]

## MORTGAGES.

Mortgage to be registered.

SECTION 60. The owner of registered land may mortgage the same by executing a mortgage deed, and such deed may be assigned, extended, discharged, released in whole or in part, or otherwise dealt with by the mortgagee by any form of deed or instrument sufficient in law for the purpose. But such mortgage deed, and all instruments assigning, extending, discharging and otherwise dealing with the mortgage, shall be registered, and shall take effect upon the title only from the time of registration.[3]

[1] Cf. § 44.                    [2] See also § 39.
[3] See § 50, and note, and cf § 57, and see next section.

SECTION 61. Registration of a mortgage shall be made in the manner following, to wit: — The owner's duplicate certificate shall be presented to the assistant recorder with the mortgage deed, and he shall enter upon the original certificate of title and also upon the owner's duplicate certificate a memorandum of the purport of the mortgage deed, the time of filing and the file number of the deed, and shall sign the memorandum. He shall also note upon the mortgage deed the time of filing and a reference to the volume and page of the registration book where it is registered. *Mortgage, how registered.*

The assistant recorder shall also, at the request of the mortgagee, make out and deliver to him a duplicate of the certificate of title, like the owner's duplicate, except that the words " Mortgagee's duplicate " shall be stamped upon it in large letters diagonally across its face. A memorandum of the issue of the mortgagee's duplicate shall be made upon the original certificate of title. *Mortgagee's duplicate.*

SECTION 62. Whenever a mortgage upon which a mortgagee's duplicate has been issued is assigned, extended, or otherwise dealt with, the mortgagee's duplicate shall be presented with the instrument assigning, extending or otherwise dealing with the mortgage, and a memorandum of the instrument shall be made upon the mortgagee's duplicate certificate. When the mortgage is discharged or otherwise extinguished the mortgagee's duplicate certificate shall be surrendered and stamped " cancelled." The production of the mortgagee's duplicate certificate shall be conclusive authority to register the instrument therewith presented, subject *Assignment or discharge of mortgage.*

however to all the provisions and exceptions contained in section fifty-six of this act so far as the same are applicable.[1]

A mortgage on registered land may be discharged[2] by the mortgagee in person on the registration book, in the same manner as a mortgage on unregistered land may be discharged by an entry on the record book in the registry of deeds, and such discharge shall be attested by an assistant recorder.

**Foreclosure of mortgage.**

SECTION 63. Mortgages of registered land may be foreclosed like mortgages of unregistered land; but in case of foreclosure by entry and possession the certificate of entry required by section two of chapter one hundred and eighty-one of the Public Statutes[3] shall be filed and registered by an assistant recorder within thirty days after the entry, in lieu of recording. After possession has been obtained by the mortgagee or his assigns, by entry or by action, and continued for the time required by law to complete the foreclosure, he or his assigns may petition the court of registration for the entry of a new certificate, and the court, after notice to all parties in interest, shall have jurisdiction to hear the cause, and may order the entry of a new certificate on such terms as equity and justice may require.

**Under Pub. Sts. ch. 181.**

In case of foreclosure by action as provided in chapter one hundred and eighty-one of the Public

---

[1] See also § 107, ¶ 3.　　[2] Or otherwise dealt with, § 60.

[3] Pub. Sts. c. 181, § 2, provides, in substance, that where entry is made for breach of condition in a mortgage, a certificate of entry shall be made on the mortgage deed, or a certificate of two witnesses to the entry shall be sworn to, such certificate to be recorded within thirty days.

Statutes, and by exercising the power of sale in the mortgage under the direction of the court as provided therein, a certified copy of the final decree of the court confirming the sale may be filed with the assistant recorder, after the time for appealing therefrom has expired,[1] and the purchaser shall thereupon be entitled to the entry of a new certificate.

*Under power of sale.*

In case of foreclosure by exercising the power of sale without a previous decree of court, the affidavit required by section eighteen of chapter one hundred and eighty-one of the Public Statutes[2] shall be filed and registered with the assistant recorder, in lieu of recording. The purchaser at the foreclosure sale or his assigns may thereupon at any time present the deed under the power of sale to the assistant recorder for filing and registration, and obtain a new certificate, the owner's duplicate certificate and the mortgagee's duplicate, if any, being first delivered up and cancelled : *provided, however*, that nothing contained in this act shall be construed to prevent the mortgagor or other person in interest from directly impeaching, by bill in equity or otherwise, any foreclosure proceedings affecting registered land, prior to the entry of a new certificate of title.

*Pub. Sts. ch. 181, § 18.*

*Bill to set aside sale.*

After a new certificate of title has been entered no judgment recovered on the mortgage note for any balance due thereon shall operate to open the foreclosure or affect the title to registered land.[3]

---

[1] Sec §§ 14, 16.

[2] Pub. Sts. ch. 181, § 18, provides, in effect, that the person selling pursuant to the power of sale contained in a mortgagee deed may, within thirty days after the sale, record his affidavit, which shall, if so recorded, be evidence that the power was duly executed.

[3] See Wing *v.* Hayford, 124 Mass. 249; Jones on Mortgages, § 1227;

## LEASES.

Leases.
SECTION 64. Leases of registered land for a term of seven years or more shall be registered in lieu of recording.[1] A lessee's duplicate certificate may be issued to the lessee upon his request, subject to the provisions hereinbefore made in regard to a mortgagee's duplicate certificate, so far as the same are applicable.[2]

## TRUSTS.

Trusts
SECTION 65. Whenever a deed or other instrument is filed for the purpose of transferring registered land in trust, or upon any equitable condition or limitation expressed therein, or for the purpose of creating or declaring a trust or other equitable interest in such land without transfer, the particulars of the trust, condition, limitation, or other equitable interest shall not be entered on the certificate; but a memorandum thereof shall be entered by the words "in trust," or "upon condition," or other apt words, and by a reference by number to the instrument authorizing or creating the same. A similar memorandum shall be made upon the duplicate certificate. The assistant recorder shall note upon the original instrument creating or declaring the trust or other equitable interest a reference by number to the certificate of title to which it relates, and to the volume and page in the registration book where it is registered. If the instru-

Memorandum to be entered.

Reference.

also Worcester, &c. Bank v. Thayer, 136 Mass. 459, and ch. 203 of the Acts of 1896 (amending Pub. Sts. ch. 181, § 42), which changed the law of Massachusetts as to sales under power of sale mortgages.

[1] Pub. Sts. ch. 120, § 4.        [2] See §§ 62, 107, ¶ 3.

ment creating or declaring a trust or other equitable
interest is already recorded in the registry of deeds
or of probate, a certified copy may be filed by the Copy.
assistant recorder and registered.

SECTION 66.   If the instrument creating or de- Power of sale.
claring a trust or other equitable interest con-
tains an express power to sell, mortgage, or deal
with the land in any manner, such power shall
be stated in the certificate of title by the words
" with power to sell," or " with power to mortgage," and by apt words of description in case of
other powers.   No instrument transferring, mort-
gaging, or in any way dealing with registered land
held in trust shall be registered, unless the power
thereto enabling is expressly conferred in the instrument of trust, or unless the decree of a court
of competent jurisdiction on a bill for instructions
or other proceeding has construed the instrument
in favor of the power, in which case a certified
copy of such decree may be filed with the assistant recorder, and he shall make registration in
accordance therewith.

This section makes the recorder the sole judge of the
validity and sufficiency of the power in question.   See note
to § 50.

SECTION 67.   When a new trustee of registered Appointment
land is appointed by the supreme judicial court or of new trustee.
the superior or probate court, a new certificate shall
be entered to him upon presentation to the assistant recorder of a certified copy of the decree and
the surrender of the duplicate certificate.[1]

[1] *Semble*, this should not be done until after the time for an appeal
from the decree of appointment has expired.

**Implied or constructive trust.**

SECTION 68. Whoever claims an interest in registered land by reason of any implied or constructive trust shall file for registration a statement thereof with the assistant recorder. The statement shall contain a description of the land, and a reference to the number of the certificate of title and the volume and page of the registration book where it is entered. Such claim shall not affect the title of a purchaser for value and in good faith before its registration.

**Trustee may apply for registration.**

SECTION 69. Any trustee shall have authority to file an application for registration of any land held in trust by him, unless expressly prohibited by the instrument creating the trust.[1]

## LEGAL INCIDENTS OF REGISTERED LAND.

**Land to remain subject to legal incidents.**

SECTION 70. Registered land, and ownership therein, shall in all respects be subject to the same burdens and incidents which attach by law to unregistered land.[2] Nothing contained in this act shall in any way be construed to relieve registered land or the owners thereof from any rights incident to the relation of husband and wife, or from liability to attachment on mesne process,[3] or levy on execution, or from liability to any lien of any description established by law on land and the buildings thereon, or the interest of the owner in such land or buildings, or to change the laws of descent, or the rights of partition between coparceners and other co-tenants, or the right to take the same by eminent domain,[4] or to relieve such

---

[1] See § 19.        [2] Cf. § 46.
[3] See §§ 73–76.      [4] See §§ 90, 91.

land from liability to be recovered by an assignee in insolvency[1] under the provisions of law relating to preferences, or to change or affect in any way any other rights or liabilities created by law and applicable to unregistered land, except as otherwise expressly provided in this act or any amendment hereof.

*Quære*, whether this supersedes the provision of § 14 and § 38, which apparently cut off rights of husband and wife in the absence of fraud if no appeal is claimed within thirty days of entering of decree. But, *semble*, these provisions would not affect the rights of a husband or wife in case of marriage after registration. See § 39, clause sixth, which preserves such rights if they attach during the proceedings, but cuts them off by inference if they attach subsequent to registration, even though before the next transaction. There is therefore here an apparent inconsistency; and the question arises, How shall such right be established and preserved? No method is prescribed, and as buyers and mortgagees will not care to assume any risk in such matters, they will be forced in the absence of satisfactory proof that no such rights exist to reject titles if they have any suspicion that there are such claims. Gibbs *v.* Messer, *supra.*

Both *dower* and *curtesy* were abolished by the English Land Transfer Bill of 1889, and by the South Australia Inheritance Act, and have also been absolutely abolished in the following States: Indiana, Iowa, Minnesota, Kansas, California, Nevada, Colorado, Washington, the Dakotas, Idaho, Wyoming, Utah, Missouri, and Arizona. See Stimson's American Statute Law, Vol. I. p. 418, § 3202 (B). The abolition of these feudal interests in land is desirable on general grounds, but would seem especially advisable, if indeed not necessary, in the case of registered land, if the land is to be a quick asset, and the registered owner to have absolute power of disposition.

[1] The insolvent law of Massachusetts was superseded by the Act of the United States Congress entitled "An Act to establish a Uniform System of Bankruptcy throughout the United States," being ch. 171 of the Laws of 1898, and which took effect July 1, 1898.

### ATTACHMENTS AND OTHER LIENS.

Attachments and liens to be registered.

SECTION 71. In every case where a writing of any description or a copy of any writ is required by law to be filed or recorded in the registry of deeds in order to create or preserve any lien, right, or attachment upon unregistered land, such writing or copy when intended to affect registered land, in lieu of recording, shall be filed and registered[1] in the office of the assistant recorder for the same registry district in which the land lies, and, in addition to any particulars required in such papers for recording with records of deeds, shall also, except in the case of attachment on mesne process,[2] contain a reference to the number of the certificate of title of the land to be affected, and the volume and page of the registration book where the certificate is registered, and also, if the attachment, right, or lien is not claimed on all the land in any certificate of title, a description sufficiently accurate for identification of the land intended to be affected.

Notice of attachment or lien.

SECTION 72. In every case where an attachment or other lien or adverse claim of any description is registered, and the duplicate certificate is not presented at the time of registration to the assistant recorder, he shall within twenty-four hours thereafter send notice by mail to the registered owner, stating that such paper has been registered, and requesting him to send or produce his duplicate certificate in order that a memorandum of the attachment, or other lien or adverse claim, may be

---

[1] See § 56.          [2] See §§ 73–76.

made thereon. If the owner neglects or refuses to comply within a reasonable time the assistant recorder shall suggest the fact to the court, and the court after notice shall enter an order to the owner to produce his certificate at a time and place to be named therein, and may enforce the order by suitable process.

SECTION 73. Attachments on mesne process [1] and liens of every description upon registered land shall be continued, reduced, discharged, and dissolved by any method sufficient in law to continue, reduce, discharge, or dissolve like liens on unregistered land. All certificates or other instruments which are permitted or required by law to be recorded in the registry of deeds to give effect to the continuance, reduction, discharge or dissolution of attachments or other liens upon unregistered lands, or to give notice of such continuance, reduction, discharge, or dissolution, shall in the case of like liens upon registered land be filed with the assistant recorder and registered [2] in the registration book, in lieu of recording. *Continuance and discharge of attachments and liens.*

SECTION 74. All the provisions of law now in force relating to attachments of real estate and leasehold estates on mesne process shall apply to registered land, except that the duties required to be performed by the register of deeds shall be performed by the asistant recorder for the registry district where the land lies, who, in lieu of recording, shall register the facts now required to be recorded, and for that purpose shall keep books similar to those now required to be kept for *Laws on attachments to remain.*

---

[1] See §§ 70, 71.      [2] See § 56.

attachments by registers of deeds, and the fees
for registering attachments shall be the same as
are now provided for recording.

**Plaintiff's attorney.** SECTION 75. The name and address of the
plaintiff's attorney shall in all cases be indorsed
upon the writ, where an attachment is made, and
he shall be deemed to be the attorney of the
plaintiff until written notice that he has ceased
to be such shall be filed for registration by the
plaintiff.

**Certificate of order, judgment, etc.** SECTION 76. Whenever an attachment on mesne
process is continued, reduced, dissolved, or other-
wise affected by an order, decision, or judgment of
the court in which the action or proceeding in
which said attachment was made is pending, or
by any order of a court of insolvency,[1] a certificate of the entry of such order, decision, or judgment from the clerk or register and under the seal
of the court, shall be entitled to be registered on
presentation to the assistant recorder. A like certificate of the allowance by the court of an amendment which a subsequent attaching creditor or
purchaser contends had the effect of dissolving an
attachment may be registered as an amendment
allowed,[2] but shall not be conclusive of dissolution,
unless the court in which the action or suit is
pending adjudicates that the amendment dissolved
the attachment, in which case a certificate of the
order, as soon as it becomes absolute, shall be registered as a dissolution of the attachment.

---

[1] See § 70, note 4.  *Quære* whether the U. S. District Court sitting in
bankruptcy is a " court of insolvency " within the meaning of this Act ?
[2] See § 23.

SECTION 77. When a mechanic's lien or lien for labor and materials is claimed upon registered and unregistered land, and the original statement required by section six of chapter one hundred and ninety-one of the Public Statutes,[1] and amendments thereof, is deposited with the register of deeds and recorded, an attested copy of such statement shall be filed with the assistant recorder and registered. *Mechanic's lien, etc.*

SECTION 78. A lien of any description upon registered land shall be enforced in the same manner as like liens upon unregistered land.[2] Whenever registered land is set off or sold on execution; or taken or sold for taxes, or for any assessment; or sold to enforce a lien for labor or materials; or the lien of a mortgagee or cotenant arising from a payment of taxes; or for an assessment under sections eleven to thirteen of chapter fifty-one of the Public Statutes,[3] or any act in amendment *Enforcement of liens.*

[1] Ch. 191, § 6, as amended by Acts of 1892, ch. 191, provides, in substance, that liens on buildings and land shall be dissolved unless a statement is filed in the registry of deeds within thirty days; and also that an inaccurate statement shall not be invalid unless intentional or misleading.

[2] See Pub. Sts. ch. 191.

[3] Pub. Sts. ch. 51, §§ 11–13.

§ 11, as amended by Acts of 1885, ch. 299, provides, in substance, that when in a city a board of public officers passes an order to lay out or alter a public way or to make any other public improvement, for a portion of which assessments may be made upon real estate, the clerk of the board shall within ten days file a declaration thereof in the registry of deeds. Notice of such assessment shall within three months be given to the party to be charged, who, under ch. 158 of Acts of 1896, may have the same apportioned into not more than ten equal parts, payable annually.

§ 12 provides, in brief, that the clerk's declaration shall state the action of the board, the intention to make such assessment, and shall specify the land to be assessed.

§ 13 reads: "No such assessment shall be laid upon any real estate except such as abuts upon streets so specified; and no such assessment shall constitute a lien upon real estate unless such declaration has been so filed."

thereof; or for costs and charges for taking down
dangerous structures under section seventeen of
chapter four hundred and eighty-one of the acts
of the year eighteen hundred and ninety-four,[1] or
any act in amendment thereof; or for erecting
fences along the line of a railroad corporation
under section one hundred and sixteen of chapter
one hundred and twelve of the Public Statutes;[2]
or for improving meadows and swamps under sections four to seven of chapter one hundred and
eighty-nine of the Public Statutes;[3] or for flowing
land under section twenty-two of chapter one hundred and ninety of the Public Statutes;[4] or for
any costs and charges incident to such liens; any
execution or copy of the execution, any officer's
return, or any deed, demand, certificate or affidavit, or other instrument made in the course of
proceedings to enforce such liens and required by

[1] § 17 of ch. 481 of the Acts of 1894 provides that, if the report of the
board of survey declares a structure to be unsafe and dangerous, and if
the owner still refuses or neglects to remove it or to make it safe, it may
be taken down or otherwise made safe, the costs incurred to constitute
a lien upon the estate.

[2] Pub. Sts. ch. 112, § 116, provides, in substance, that when the duty of
maintaining a fence along a railroad rests upon a person other than the
corporation, the latter shall erect or repair such fence, and have a lien
upon the land for the recovery from such person of the reasonable cost
therefor.

[3] Pub. Sts. ch. 189, §§ 4-7, provide, in effect, that when, after petition
and hearing, commissioners are appointed for improving meadows, swamps,
and other low land, they may direct such changes to be made as they may
deem most beneficial.   Under § 5 they may employ suitable persons to perform the work; under § 6 shall assess the whole charge among the pro-
prietors of the lands; and under § 7 may appoint a collector of the money
assessed.

[4] Pub. Sts. ch. 190, § 22, provides, in substance, that, where damages have
been awarded for the overflow or injury otherwise sustained by the erection
of a mill dam, the person entitled to the damages shall have a lien therefor
on the mill, the mill dam, and the land used therewith.

law to be recorded in the registry of deeds in the case of unregistered land, shall be filed with the assistant recorder for the district where the land lies,[1] and registered in the registration book, and a memorandum made upon the proper certificate of title in each case as an adverse claim or encumbrance.

SECTION 79. Upon the expiration of the time allowed by law for redemption after registered land has been set off or sold on any execution,[2] or taken or sold for the enforcement of any lien of any description, the person claiming under an execution, or under any deed or other instrument made in the course of proceedings to levy such execution or enforce any lien, may petition the court for the entry of a new certificate to him, and the application may be granted: *provided, however*, that every new certificate entered under this section shall contain a memorandum of the nature of the proceeding on which it is based; and *provided, further*, that where a new certificate is entered in pursuance of any tax title such certificate shall contain a memorandum that it is subject to the rights of redemption reserved in sections fifty-seven and seventy-six of chapter three hundred and ninety of the acts of the year eighteen hundred and eighty-eight,[3] or any acts

*After non-redemption lien-holder may get certificate.*

*Act of 1888, ch. 390, §§ 57, 76.*

[1] See § 41, *Proviso.*
[2] See Pub. Sts. ch. 172, §§ 31, 32.
[3] § 57 of ch. 390 of the Acts of 1888 provides that the owner of real estate taken or sold for payment of taxes may redeem the property within two years from the day of taking or sale. Section 76 reads: "In all cases of taking or sale of real estate for the payment of taxes assessed thereon, the supreme judicial court shall have equity powers, if relief is sought within five years from the taking or sale."

in amendment thereof or in substitution therefor, and *provided, further*, that at any time prior to the entry of a new certificate the registered owner may pursue all his legal and equitable remedies to impeach or annul proceedings under executions or to enforce liens of any description.

This provision for noting in the certificate matters or facts upon which the order for the certificate is based appears here for the first time. The registration of title in the first instance is not required to contain any such statements. See §§ 38 and 49.

## PENDING SUITS, JUDGMENTS, DECREES, AND PARTITIONS.

Memorandum of suits, judgments, etc., to be registered.

SECTION 80. No writ of entry, petition for partition, or other action at law, or any proceeding in equity affecting the title to real estate or the use and occupation thereof, or the buildings thereon, and no judgment or decree, nor any writ of error, bill of review or other proceeding to vacate or reverse any judgment or decree, shall have any effect upon registered land as against persons other than the parties thereto, unless a memorandum like that described in section thirteen of chapter one hundred and twenty-six of the Public Statutes,[1] and amendments thereof, containing also a reference to the number of the certificate of title of

[1] Pub. Sts. ch. 126, § 13, as amended by Acts of 1897, ch. 463, provides, in effect, that "No writ of entry, petition for partition, or other proceeding either at law or in equity, affecting the title to real estate, or the use and occupation thereof or the buildings thereon," shall bind third parties without notice until a memorandum is recorded in the registry of deeds. The section does not, however, apply to attachments, levies of execution, or proceedings in the probate courts.

By ch. 289 of the Acts of 1892 this section was extended to judgments and decrees.

the land affected, and the volume and page of the registration book where it is entered, shall be filed and registered. This section shall not apply *Exceptions.* to attachments, levies of execution, or to proceedings for the probate of wills, or for administration, in the probate court: *provided, however*, that in case notice of the pendency of the action has been duly registered it shall be sufficient to register the judgment or decree in such action within sixty days after the rendition thereof.

SECTION 81. At any time after final judgment *Certificate under Pub. Sts. ch. 126, § 14, may be registered.* or decree in favor of the defendant, or other disposition in the manner specified in section fourteen of chapter one hundred and twenty-six of the Public Statutes,[1] of any case in which a memorandum has been registered as provided in the preceding section, a certificate of the clerk stating the manner of disposal thereof, as provided in said section fourteen, shall be entitled to registration.

SECTION 82. Whenever in any real action *Judgment may be registered.* affecting registered land judgment is entered for the plaintiff or demandant, except in actions of ejectment and actions under chapter one hundred and seventy-five of the Public Statutes,[2] relating to terms of less than seven years, such judgment shall be entitled to registration on presentation of

---

[1] Pub. Sts. ch. 126, § 14, provides that, at any time after final judgment or decree in favor of the defendant, or other final disposition of a proceeding in a writ of entry, petition for partition, or other proceeding, either at law or in equity, affecting the title to real estate, or the use and occupation thereof or the buildings thereon, or in case of the non-entry of the writ, petition, or bill of complaint, the clerk of the court shall, on demand, give a certificate of such final disposition, or non-entry, which certificate may be recorded.

[2] Pub. Sts. ch. 175, "Of the Summary Process for the Recovery of Land."

a certificate of the entry thereof from the clerk
of the court where the action is pending, to the
assistant recorder, who shall enter a memorandum
upon the certificate of title of the land to which
such judgment relates.  If the judgment does not
apply to all the land described in the certificate
of title, the certificate of the clerk and the memorandum entered by the assistant recorder shall
contain a description of the land affected by the
judgment.

Writ of entry.     SECTION 83.  When in any writ of entry an
execution or writ of seizin has been issued and
served by the officer, he shall cause an attested
copy of the execution, with a return of his doings
thereon, to be filed and registered within three
months after the service and before the return of
the execution into the clerk's office, and the demandant, in case the judgment was that he was
entitled to an estate in fee simple in the demanded
premises, or in any part thereof, and for which
execution issued, shall thereupon be entitled to
the entry of a new certificate of title : *provided*,
that in informations under chapter one hundred
Pub. Sts. ch.   and eighty-two of the Public Statutes[1] the Com-
182.
monwealth shall be entitled to have the certificate
of the registered owner cancelled by the court of
registration as soon as judgment is rendered in its
favor.

Writ of dower     SECTION 84.  When in a writ of dower judg-
or waste.
ment is entered confirming the report of the commissioners under section seven of chapter one

---

[1] Pub. Sts. ch. 182, " Of Information for Intrusion and for the Recovery
of Lands by the Commonwealth."

hundred and seventy-four of the Public Statutes,[1] or when in a writ of waste[2] judgment is entered that the plaintiff recover the place wasted, a certificate of the entry of such judgment may be registered as an encumbrance.

SECTION 85. Any decree of a court of equity affecting title or rights in registered land, whether made in the exercise of general equity jurisdiction, or in the exercise of jurisdiction conferred by statute for the quieting of titles or removing clouds from titles, as in chapter two hundred and thirty-seven of the acts of the year eighteen hundred and eighty-two, chapter two hundred and eighty-three of the acts of the year eighteen hundred and eighty-five, chapter four hundred and forty-two of the acts of the year eighteen hundred and eighty-nine, and chapter three hundred and forty of the acts of the year eighteen hundred and ninety-three, or of any similar purpose, may be registered in the same manner as a judgment at law. But every court of equity passing such a decree shall, upon application of the plaintiff or petitioner, order any parties before it to execute for registration any deed or instrument necessary to give effect to its decree,[3] and may require the registered owner to deliver his duplicate certificate[4] to the plaintiff or petitioner to be cancelled, or to have a memorandum entered upon it by the assistant

*Decree affecting title may be registered.*

*Necessary deeds to be executed.*

---

[1] Pub. Sts. ch. 174, § 7, relating to the writ of dower, provides that the commissioners appointed to set out dower shall make return to the court of their doings, and if their report be confirmed, judgment shall be rendered that the assignment of dower shall be effectual during the life of the demandant.

[2] See Pub. Sts. ch. 179.

[3] See § 17.          [4] See § 72.

recorder. In case the person required to execute any deed or other instrument necessary to give effect to the decree is absent from the Commonwealth, or is a minor, or insane, or for any reason not amenable to the process of the court, the court may appoint some suitable person a trustee to execute such instrument, and the same when executed shall be registered and shall have full force and effect to bind the land to be affected thereby.

Ch. 237 of the Acts of 1882 provides that when the record title of real estate is encumbered by an undischarged mortgage, and the mortgagor and those having his estate in the premises have been in uninterupted possession for twenty years after full performance thereof, he or they may petition the Supreme Judicial Court to enter a decree discharging the mortgage. This act was —

Extended by ch. 283 of the Acts of 1885 to a mortgage given to secure the mortgagee against some contingent liability which has ceased to exist; and was —

Amended by § 1 of ch. 427 of the Acts of 1890, in order to allow the petition to be filed by any person having a freehold estate or any interest in the land, or in any part thereof, and also to allow two or more persons owning in severalty different portions or interests in the whole or in different portions to join in one petition.

Ch. 442 of the Acts of 1889, "An Act to provide for Determining the Validity, Nature, or Extent of certain Encumbrances upon Titles to Real Estate," provides that when the record title to land is affected by conditions, restrictions, etc., made more than thirty years ago, a petition may be made to the Supreme Judicial Court for the purpose of determining the nature or validity of such possible encumbrances. Two or more defects may be set forth in the same petition, and when the names of the respondents are unknown, proceedings against them may be had by a general description. The decree of the court shall exclude all respondents from any claim contrary to its determination, and shall have the effect of a release of such claims executed by the respondents in due form of law. Section 2 of ch. 427 of the Acts of 1890 authorizes the joinder of two or more persons in a petition under this chapter.

Ch. 340 of the Acts of 1893, "An Act relative to Quieting Title to Real Estate," provides that when the record title to property is clouded by an adverse claim, or by the possibility of such claim, petition may be made to the Supreme Judicial Court praying that such claimants may be summoned to show cause why they should not bring action to try such claim. Where no better description can be given, a general description shall suffice.

Ch. 522 of the Acts of 1897, as amended by ch. 457 of the Acts of 1898, provides that in any suit in equity brought to quiet or establish the title to real estate situated within the Commonwealth, or to remove a cloud from the title, in which suit it is sought to determine the claims or rights of any person or persons unknown, unascertained, not in being, or out of the Commonwealth, or who cannot be actually served with process, they may be made parties defendant, and general words of description, such as the heirs or legal representatives of A. B., or such persons as shall become heirs, devisees, or appointees of C. D., a living person claiming under A. B., shall suffice. And it shall be sufficient for the maintenance of such suit that the parties defendant claim or may claim by purchase, descent, or otherwise, some right, title, interest, or estate in the land, which claim cannot be met by the plaintiffs without the production of evidence. Two or more persons claiming separate parcels in the same county by titles derived from a common source may join as parties plaintiff. In certain cases the court may of its own motion appoint guardians *ad litem* or next friends.

For comment upon the essence of these provisions, see note to § 35, and Loring *v.* Hildreth, *supra*.

SECTION 86. In all proceedings for partition of registered land, or for the assignment in fee of registered land claimed by husband or wife by stat- *Proceedings for partition or assignment of marital rights under statutes.*

utory right,[1] after the entry of the final judgment
or decree of partition and the acceptance of the
report of the commissioners, a copy of the judgment or decree and of the return of the commissioners, certified by the clerk or register, as the
case may be, shall be filed and registered; and
thereupon, in case the land is set off to the owners
in severalty, any owner shall be entitled to have a
certificate entered of the share set off to him in severalty, and to receive an owner's duplicate therefor.   In case the land is ordered by the court to be
sold, the purchaser or his assigns shall be entitled
to have a certificate of title entered to him or them
on presenting the deed of the commissioners for
registration : *provided, however*, that any new certificate entered in pursuance of partition proceedings, whether by way of set off or of sale, shall
contain a reference to the final judgment or decree
of partition, and shall be conclusive as to the title
to the same extent and against the same persons
as such judgment or decree is made conclusive by
the statutes applicable thereto ;[2] and *provided, also*,
that any person holding such certificate of title or a
transfer thereof shall have the right to petition the
court at any time to cancel the memorandum relating to such judgment or decree, and the court, after
notice and hearing, may grant the application.
Such certificate shall thereafter be conclusive in
the same manner and to the same extent as other
certificates of title.

Mortgage or
lease registered
prior to parti-
tion to be in-
dorsed.

SECTION 87.   When a certified copy of a judgment or decree for partition and of the return of

[1] See Pub. Sts. ch. 124, and amendments.   And see note to § 70.
[2] See Pub. Sts. ch. 178, and amendments.

the commissioners is presented for registration, if
a mortgage or lease affecting a specific portion
or an undivided share of the premises had previously been registered, the tenant claiming under
the mortgagor [1] or lessor [2] shall cause the mortgage
or lease and any duplicate certificate of title issued
to the mortgagee or lessee to be again presented
for registration, and the assistant recorder shall
indorse on each a memorandum of such partition,
with a description of the land set off in severalty
on which such mortgage or lease remains in force.
Such tenant shall not be entitled to receive his own
duplicate certificate of title until such mortgage
or lease has been so presented for registration. [3]

INSOLVENCY.

SECTION 88. It shall be the duty of the messenger to register notice of the issuing of a warrant in insolvency [4] against a debtor who is an
owner of registered land, when the same is committed to him, by filing a copy thereof with the
assistant recorder.

An assignee in insolvency [5] shall be entitled to
the entry of a new certificate of registered land
of the debtor upon presenting and filing a certified
copy of the assignment, with the insolvent's duplicate certificate of title; but the new certificate
shall state that it is entered to him as assignee in
insolvency.

SECTION 89. Whenever proceedings in insolvency against a registered owner of which notice

[1] See § 60.  [2] See § 64.  [3] See note to § 27.
[4] See § 70, note.  [5] See § 107.

has been registered are vacated by decree, or when the court of insolvency grants a discharge and orders a reconveyance of land to an insolvent debtor in proceedings under chapter two hundred and thirty-six of the acts of the year eighteen hundred and eighty-four,[1] and acts in amendment thereof, a certified copy of the decree, or of such discharge and order, may be filed and registered. If a new certificate has been entered to the assignee in insolvency as registered owner the debtor shall be entitled to the entry of a new certificate to him, and the certificate of the assignee shall be surrendered.

## EMINENT DOMAIN.

Eminent do-
main.

SECTION 90. Whenever any land of a registered owner, or any right or interest therein, is taken by eminent domain,[2] the Commonwealth or body politic or corporate or other authority exercising such right shall file for registration in the proper registry district a description of the registered land so taken, giving the name of each owner thereof,[3] referring by number and place of registration in the registration book to each certificate of title, and stating what estate or interest in the land is taken, and for what purpose. A memorandum of the right or interest taken shall be made on each certificate of title by the assistant recorder, and where the fee simple is taken a new certificate shall be entered to the owner for the land remaining to him

---

[1] See Acts of 1884, ch. 236, and note to § 70.

[2] See § 70.

[3] This changes the existing law. See Woodbury v. Marblehead, &c. Co., 145 Mass. 509.

after such taking. In any case where the owner has a lien upon the land taken for his damages it shall be so stated in the memorandum of registration. All fees on account of any memorandum of registration or entry of new certificates shall be paid by the Commonwealth or body politic or corporate or other authority taking the land.

SECTION 91. When for any reason, by operation of law, land which was taken for a public use reverts to the owner from whom it was taken or to his heirs or assigns, the court upon the petition of the person entitled to the benefit of the reversion, after notice and hearing, may order the entry of a new certificate of title to him.

*Reversion of land taken by eminent domain.*

## TRANSFER BY DESCENT OR DEVISE.

SECTION 92. Upon the death of a registered owner his heirs at law or devisees on the expiration of thirty days after the entry of a decree of the probate court granting letters testamentary or of administration, or in case of an appeal from such decree, at any time after the entry of a final decree,[1] may file a certified copy of the final decree of the probate court and of the will, if any, with the assistant recorder, and make application for the entry of a new certificate. The court shall issue notice to the executor and administrator and all other persons in interest, and may also give notice by publication in such newspaper or newspapers as it may deem proper, to all whom it may concern,[2] and after hearing may direct the entry

*Transfer of land by descent or devise.*

[1] See Haddock v. Boston & Maine R. R., 146 Mass. 155, and Acts of 1889, ch. 435.

[2] See § 32, note, and §§ 35, 38, and 109.

of a new certificate or certificates to the person or
persons entitled as heirs or devisees. Any new
certificate so entered before the final settlement of
the estate of the deceased owner in the probate
court shall state expressly that it is entered by
transfer from the last certificate by descent or devise, and that the estate is in process of settlement.
After the final settlement of the estate in the
probate court, or after the expiration of the time
allowed by law for bringing an action against an
executor or administrator by creditors of the deceased,[1] the heirs at law or devisees may petition
the court for an order to cancel the memorandum
upon their certificate, stating that the estate is in
course of settlement, and the court, after notice[2]
and hearing, may grant the petition: *provided,
however*, that the liability of heirs or devisees of
registered land for claims against the estate of the
deceased shall not in any way be diminished or
changed.[3]

Executor, ad-
ministrator, or
guardian may
sell or mort-
gage under
license.

SECTION 93.   Nothing contained in this act shall
in any way affect or impair the jurisdiction of the
probate court to license an executor or administrator or guardian to sell or mortgage registered land
for any purpose for which a license may be granted
in the case of unregistered land.   The purchaser
or mortgagee taking a deed executed in pursuance
of such license shall be entitled to a new certificate
of title, or memorandum of registration, on presenting his deed to the assistant recorder.

[1] See Pub. Sts. ch. 136.
[2] What notice ? by publication, or mailing, or what ?
[3] Pub. Sts. ch. 136, §§ 26-32.

## ASSURANCE FUND.

SECTION 94. Upon the original registration of land under this act, and also upon the entry of a certificate showing title as registered owners in heirs or devisees, there shall be paid to the recorder one tenth of one per cent of the assessed value of the real estate,[1] on the basis of the last assessment for municipal taxation, as an assurance fund.

*Assurance fund.*

SECTION 95. All money received by the recorder under the preceding section shall be paid to the treasurer of the Commonwealth. He shall keep the same invested, with the advice and approval of the governor and council, and shall report annually to the general court the condition and income thereof.

*Treasurer of Commonwealth to manage assurance fund.*

SECTION 96. Any person who without negligence on his part sustains loss or damage, or is deprived of land or of any estate or interest therein after the original registration of land under this act,[2] by the registration of any other person as owner of such land or of any estate or interest therein, through fraud or in consequence of any error, omission, mistake, or misdescription in any certificate of title or in any entry or memorandum in the registration book, may bring and prosecute an action of contract in the superior court for the recovery of compensation for such loss or damage or for such land or estate or interest therein, from the assurance fund: *provided, however,* that where

*Action for loss or damage to land.*

*Provisos.*

---

[1] See note 3, § 21.

[2] This section, if literally construed, will cut off all right to compensation on the part of any person injured by the original registration. See § 14; cf. § 97.

the person deprived of land or of any estate or interest therein in the manner above stated has right of action or other remedy for the recovery of the land or of the estate or interest therein, he shall exhaust such right of action or other remedy before resorting to the action of contract herein provided; and *provided, further*, that nothing in this act shall be construed to deprive the plaintiff of any action of tort which he may have against any person for such loss or damage, or deprivation of land or of any estate or interest therein. But if the plaintiff elects to pursue his remedy in tort, and also brings an action of contract under this act, the action of contract shall be continued to await the result of the action of tort.[1]

*Against whom action lies.*

SECTION 97. If such action of contract is brought to recover for loss or damage or for deprivation of land or of any estate or interest therein, arising wholly through any fraud, negligence, omission, mistake, or misfeasance of the recorder, assistant recorder, or of any of the examiners of title, in the performance of executive or ministerial duties, or of any of the assistants or clerks of the recorder, in the performance of their respective duties, then the action shall be brought against the treasurer of the Commonwealth as sole defendant.[2]

If such action is brought to recover for loss or damage or deprivation of land or of any estate or interest therein arising wholly through any fraud,

---

[1] See § 55, and also § 103. Observe that in Massachusetts ejectment and writs of entry fall within the category of actions of tort, the right to use which is carefully preserved in this section.

[2] Ibid.

negligence, omission, mistake, or misfeasance of
some person or persons other than the recorder,
assistant recorder, or the other officers and assistants above named, or arising jointly through the
fraud, negligence, omission, mistake, or misfeasance of such other person and the recorder, assistant recorder, or other officers and assistants above
named, then such action shall be brought against
both the treasurer of the Commonwealth and such
other person or persons, as joint defendants.

SECTION 98. Where there are defendants other
than the treasurer of the Commonwealth, and
where judgment is entered for the plaintiff against
the treasurer and against some or all of the other
defendants, execution shall issue against the other
defendants and be levied upon them. If the execution is returned unsatisfied in whole or in part,
and the officer returning the same certifies that
the amount due cannot be collected from the lands
or goods of such other defendants, a justice of the
superior court shall direct the clerk to certify to
the governor the amount due on the execution,
and the governor shall draw his warrant therefor
upon the treasurer of the Commonwealth, and the
treasurer shall pay the amount out of the assurance fund, without any further act or resolve
making an appropriation therefor.

When in such action judgment for any reason
cannot be entered against all or any of the other
defendants, it may be entered against the treasurer
alone, or against the treasurer and such of the
other defendants as are found to be liable, and
against whom judgment can lawfully be entered.

5

Whenever judgment is entered against the treasurer of the Commonwealth alone, whether in a case where he is sole defendant or joint defendant with others, the justice of the superior court before whom the action is tried shall direct the clerk to transmit to the governor a certificate of the entry of judgment and of the amount due, and the treasurer shall pay the same upon the warrant of the governor, as above provided.

*Assurance fund repleted from treasury.* SECTION 99. If the assurance fund at any time is not sufficient to meet the amount called for by such warrant of the governor the treasurer shall make up the deficiency from any funds in the treasury not otherwise appropriated; and in such case any sums thereafter received by the treasurer on account of the assurance fund shall be transferred to the general funds of the treasury, until the amount paid on account of the deficiency shall have been made up.

*Commonwealth to be subrogated to rights of plaintiff.* SECTION 100. In every case where payment has been made by the treasurer of the Commonwealth under warrant from the governor, the Commonwealth shall be subrogated to all rights of the plaintiff against any other parties or securities, and the treasurer shall enforce the same in behalf of the Commonwealth. Any sums so recovered by the treasurer shall be paid into the treasury of the Commonwealth to the account of the assurance fund.

*Income of assurance fund.* SECTION 101. The income of the assurance fund shall be added to the principal and invested, until said fund amounts to the sum of two hundred thousand dollars, and thereafter the income of such fund shall be used to defray, as far as may be, the expenses of the administration of this act, instead of being added to the fund and accumulated.

SECTION 102. The assurance fund shall not be liable to pay for any loss, damage, or deprivation occasioned by a breach of trust, whether express, implied, or constructive, by any registered owner who is a trustee, or by the improper exercise of any power of sale in a mortgage. Nor shall any plaintiff recover as compensation in an action of contract under this act more than the fair market value of the real estate at the time of the last payment to the assurance fund on account of the same real estate.

*Assurance fund not liable in case of breach of trust.*

SECTION 103. All actions of contract for compensation under this act by reason of any loss or damage or deprivation of land or any estate or interest therein shall be begun within the period of six years from the time when the cause of action accrued, and not afterwards : *provided, however,* that the plaintiff in an action for the recovery of the land or estate or interest therein in accordance with section ninety-seven of this act may bring the action of contract for compensation within one year after the termination of such action ; and *provided, further,* that the action of contract herein provided shall survive to the personal representative of the registered owner, unless barred in his lifetime, but the proceeds thereof shall be treated as real estate.

*Action for compensation to be begun within six years.*

*Provisos.*

[1] See §§ 55, 96, 97 ; and *quære,* whether the reference in § 103 to § 97 is not an error for § 96, or for § 38 ?

## POWERS OF ATTORNEY.

Power of attorney.

**SECTION 104.** Any person may by attorney procure land to be registered and convey or otherwise deal with registered land,[1] but the letters of attorney shall be acknowledged and filed with the recorder or the assistant recorder of the proper registry district, and registered. Any instrument revoking such letters shall be acknowledged and registered in like manner.

## LOST DUPLICATE CERTIFICATES.

Lost duplicate certificates may be replaced.

**SECTION 105.** If a duplicate certificate is lost or destroyed, or cannot be produced by a grantee, heir, devisee, assignee, or other person, applying for the entry of a new certificate to him or for the registration of any instrument, a suggestion of the fact of such loss or destruction may be filed by the registered owner or other person in interest and registered. The court may thereupon, upon the petition of the registered owner or other person in interest, after notice and hearing, direct the issue of a new duplicate certificate, which shall contain a memorandum of the fact that it is issued in place of a lost duplicate certificate, but shall in all respects be entitled to like faith and credit as the original duplicate, and shall thereafter be regarded as the original duplicate for all the purposes of this act.

## ADVERSE CLAIMS.

Adverse claims.

**SECTION 106.** Whoever claims any right or interest in registered land adverse to the registered

---

[1] See §§ 19, 21.

owner arising subsequent to the date of original registration may, if no other provision is made in this act for registering the same, make a statement in writing setting forth fully his alleged right or interest, and how or under whom acquired, and a reference to the volume and page of the certificate of title of the registered owner, and a description of the land in which the right or interest is claimed. The statement shall be signed and sworn to, and shall state the adverse claimant's residence, and designate a place at which all notices may be served upon him. This statement shall be entitled to registration as an adverse claim, and the court, upon the petition of any party in interest, shall grant a speedy hearing upon the question of the validity of such adverse claim, and shall enter such decree thereon as justice and equity may require. If the claim is adjudged to be invalid, the registration shall be cancelled. If in any case the court after notice[1] and hearing shall find that a claim thus registered was frivolous or vexatious, it may tax the adverse claimant double costs.

## SURRENDER OF DUPLICATE CERTIFICATES.

Section 107. In every case where the recorder or any assistant recorder is requested to enter a new certificate in pursuance of an instrument purporting to be executed by the registered owner, or by reason of any instrument or proceedings which divest the title of the registered owner against his consent, if the outstanding owner's duplicate cer-

Duplicate certificates, if not surrendered, may be annulled by decree of court.

[1] See note 2, § 92.

tificate is not presented for cancellation when such request is made, the recorder or assistant recorder shall not enter a new certificate, but the person claiming to be entitled thereto may apply by petition to the court. The court, after a hearing, may order the registered owner or any person withholding the duplicate certificate to surrender the same, and direct the entry of a new certificate upon such surrender.

If in any case the person withholding the duplicate certificate is not amenable to the process of the court, or if for any reason the outstanding owner's duplicate certificate cannot be delivered up, the court may by decree annul the same, and order a new certificate of title to be entered. Such new certificate and all duplicates thereof shall contain a memorandum of the annulment of the outstanding duplicate.

If in any case an outstanding mortgagee's or lessee's duplicate certificate is not produced and surrendered when the mortgage is discharged or extinguished or the lease is terminated, like proceedings may be had to obtain registration as in the case of the non-production of an owner's duplicate.

## AMENDMENT AND ALTERATION OF CERTIFICATES OF TITLE.

No amendment or alteration of certificates shall be made except by decree of court.

SECTION 108. No erasure, alteration, or amendment shall be made upon the registration book after the entry of a certificate of title or of a memorandum thereon and the attestation of the same by the recorder or an assistant recorder, ex-

cept by order of the court. Any registered owner
or other person in interest may at any time apply
by petition to the court, upon the ground that
registered interests of any description, whether
vested, contingent, expectant, or inchoate, have
terminated and ceased ; or that new interests
have arisen or been created which do not appear
upon the certificate ; or that any error, omission,
or mistake was made in entering a certificate or
any memorandum thereon, or on any duplicate
certificate ; or that the name of any person on the
certificate has been changed ; or that the registered owner has been married, or if registered as
married that the marriage has been terminated ;
or that a corporation which owned registered land
and has been dissolved has not conveyed the same
within three years after its dissolution ; or upon
any other reasonable ground ; and the court shall
have jurisdiction to hear and determine the petition after notice to all parties in interest,[1] and
may order the entry of a new certificate, the
entry or cancellation of a memorandum upon a
certificate, or grant any other relief upon such
terms and conditions, requiring security if necessary, as it may deem proper ; *provided, however,* Proviso.
that this section shall not be construed to give
the court authority to open the original decree of
registration, and that nothing shall be done or
ordered by the court which shall impair the title
or other interest of a purchaser holding a certifi-

---

[1] The form and manner of notice seem to be left entirely to the discretion of the court. See § 35 and note. And see note 2, § 92. Cf. also
§ 109.

cate for value and in good faith, or his heirs or assigns, without his or their written consent.

Any petition filed under this section, and all petitions and motions filed under the provisions of this act after original registration, shall be filed and entitled in the original case in which the decree of registration was entered.

### SERVICE OF NOTICES AFTER REGISTRATION.

Notices after registration to be mailed.

SECTION 109. All notices required by or given in pursuance of the provisions of this act by the recorder or any assistant recorder, after original registration, shall be sent by mail to the person to be notified at his residence and post-office address as stated in the certificate of title, or in any registered instrument under which he claims an interest, in the office of the recorder or assistant recorder, relating to the parcel of land in question.

All notices and citations directed by special order of the court under the provisions of this act, after original registration, may be served in the manner above stated, and the certificate of the recorder shall be conclusive proof[1] of such service :

Proviso.

*provided, however,* that the court may in any case order different or further service, by publication or otherwise.[2]

### FEES FOR REGISTRATION.

SECTION 110. The fees payable under this act shall be as follows : —

---

[1] See § 32, note, and § 33.  [2] See § 92 and § 108.

For every application to bring land under this act, including indexing and recording the same, and transmitting to recorder, when filed with assistant recorder, three dollars. Schedule of fees for registration.

For every plan filed, seventy-five cents.

For indexing an instrument recorded while application for registration is pending, twenty-five cents.

For examining title, five dollars, and one tenth of one per cent of the value of the land.

For each notice by mail, twenty-five cents, and the actual cost of printing.

For all services by a sheriff under this act, the same fees as are now provided by law for like services.

For each notice by publication, twenty-five cents, and the actual cost of publication.

For entry of order dismissing application, or decree of registration, and sending memorandum to assistant recorder, one dollar.

For copy of decree of registration, one dollar.

For entry of original certificate of title and issuing one duplicate certificate, three dollars.

For making and entering a new certificate of title including issue of one duplicate certificate, one dollar.

For each additional duplicate certificate, after the first, fifty cents.

For the registration of every instrument, whether single or in duplicate or triplicate, including entering, indexing, and filing same, and attesting registration thereof, and also making and attesting copy of memorandum on one instrument or on a duplicate certificate when required, one dollar and fifty cents.

For making and attesting copy of memorandum on each additional instrument or duplicate certificate if required, fifty cents.

For filing and registering an adverse claim, three dollars.

For entering statement of change of residence or post-office address, including indorsing and attesting same on a duplicate certificate, twenty-five cents.

For entering any note in the entry book or in the registration book, twenty-five cents.

For the registration of a suggestion of death or notice of issue of a warrant in insolvency, twenty-five cents.

For the registration of a discharge or release of mortgage or other instrument creating an encumbrance, fifty cents.

For the registration of a memorandum or certificate of entry for possession or deposition in proof thereof, fifty cents.

For the registration of any levy, or of any discharge or dissolution of any attachment or levy, or of any certificate of or receipt for payment of taxes, or of any mechanic's lien or lien for labor or materials, or notice of any pending action or of a judgment or decree, fifty cents.

For indorsing on any mortgage, lease, or other instrument a memorandum of partition, one dollar.

For every petition filed under this act after original registration, one dollar.

For a certified copy of any decree or registered

instrument, the same fees as are provided by law for registers of deeds.

In all cases not expressly provided for by law the fees of all public officers for any official duty or service under this act shall be at the same rate as those prescribed herein for like services.

## PENALTIES.

SECTION 111. Certificates of title and duplicate certificates issued under this act shall be subjects of larceny.

*Certificates subjects of larceny.*

SECTION 112. Whoever knowingly swears falsely to any statement required to be made under oath by this act shall be guilty of perjury, and liable to the statutory penalties for perjury.

*Perjury.*

SECTION 113. A certificate of title, duplicate certificate of title, certificate issued in place of a duplicate certificate, the registration book, entry book, and all indexes provided for by this act, and the docket of the recorder, shall be treated as if specifically described and enumerated in section one of chapter two hundred and four of the Public Statutes,[1] and the various acts therein described, when done in reference to the records or instruments hereinbefore mentioned, shall be punished as provided in said section and chapter.

*Forgery of records, certificates, etc.*

*Pub. Sts. ch. 204, § 1.*

SECTION 114. Whoever forges or procures to be forged, or assists in forging, the seal of the court of registration, or stamps or procures to be

*Forging court seal.*

[1] Pub. Sts. ch. 204, § 1, on "Forgery and Offences against the Currency," provides that whoever, with intent to injure or defraud any person, forges a public record, certificate of any public officer, or any evidence or muniment of title to property, shall be punished by imprisonment in the state prison not exceeding ten years, or in jail not exceeding ten years.

stamped, or assists in stamping, any document with such forged seal, or with the genuine seal of the court of registration without being duly authorized thereto, shall be punished by imprisonment in the state prison not exceeding ten years or in the jail not exceeding two years.

**Fraudulent conveyance of encumbered land.** SECTION 115. Whoever, with intent to defraud, sells and conveys registered land knowing that an undischarged attachment or any other encumbrance exists thereon which is not noted by memorandum on the duplicate certificate of title, without informing the grantee of such attachment or other encumbrance before the consideration is paid, shall be punished by imprisonment in the state prison not exceeding three years, or in the jail not exceeding one year.

**Act to take effect Oct. 1, 1898.** SECTION 116. This act shall take effect upon the first day of October in the year eighteen hundred and ninety-eight.

[*Approved June 23, 1898.*]

# BIBLIOGRAPHY.

## AUSTRALIA.

1881. TORRENS, SIR ROBERT, K. C. M. G.,
An Essay on the Transfer of Land by Registration. Pamphlet, 12mo, pp. vi, 88. Cassell & Co., London, Paris, New York, and Melbourne.

1883. MAXWELL, W. E., COMMISSIONER OF LAND, REPORT OF, 1883,
The Torrens System of Conveyancing by Registration of Title in Adelaide and South Australia.

1890. DUFFEY AND EAGLESON,
Transfer of Land Act, 1890. G. Partridge & Co., Melbourne.

## CANADA.

1883. MASON, J. HERBERT,
Land Transfer Reform. Address before Canadian Institute, Toronto, 1883.

1886. JONES, HERBERT C.,
The Torrens System of Transfer of Land. Casswell & Co., Toronto, 1883. (Complete, with British references.)

## ENGLAND.

1832. COMMISSIONERS, REAL PROPERTY, SECOND REPORT OF, 1832.

1850. COMMISSIONERS OF REGISTRATION AND CONVEYANCING, REPORT OF, 1850.

1873. COLT, F. HOARE,
Remarks on the Land Transfer Question. Pamphlet, London, 1873.

1875. LORD CAIRNS,
Land Transfer Act of 1875.

187-. COLT, F. HOARE,
Handy Book on Registration of Title and Transfer of Land. London.

1878-9. COMMITTEE, SPECIAL, OF HOUSE OF COMMONS ON
LAND TITLES AND TRANSFER, REPORT OF,
1878-9. (Valuable.)

1879. COLONIAL AUTHORITIES, SUPPLEMENTARY RETURNS
TO HOUSE OF COMMONS BY,
System of Conveyancing by Registration of Title
in Australia, Tasmania, New Zealand, British
Columbia, and Fiji, made up to December 31,
1879. London, 1879.

1881. JEVONS, PROF. W. A.,
The Land Laws. Fortnightly Review, Vol. 35,
No. CLXXI., March, 1881.

1881. COLONIAL AUTHORITIES, RETURNS TO HOUSE OF
COMMONS BY, 1881,
Registration of Title in the British Colonies.

1883. BRODERICK, HON. GEORGE C.,
The Reform in the English Land System. London, 1883.

1883. MAINE, SIR HENRY,
Early English Law and Custom, Chap. X. Henry
Holt & Co., New York, 1883.

1885. ARGYLL, DUKE OF,
Land Reformers. Contemporary Review, October,
1885.

1885. COLT, F. HOARE,
Supplementary Suggestions on Land Transfer Question. Pamphlet, London, 1885.

1885. LEFEVRE, RT. HON. G. SHAW,
The Question of Land. Nineteenth Century, October, 1885.

1885. MARLBOROUGH, DUKE OF,
The Transfer of Land. Fortnightly Review, April,
1885.

1886. BAR COMMITTEE, BY ORDER OF,
Land Transfer. London, 1886.

1886. COUNCIL OF THE INCORPORATED LAW SOCIETY OF
LONDON,
Statement on the Land Laws. London, 1886.
1886. ELPHINSTONE, HOWARD W.,
On the Transfer of Land. 2 Law Quarterly Re-
view, January, 1886.
1886. HOBHOUSE, RT. HON. LORD,
Free Land. Contemporary Review, Part I., Feb-
ruary, 1886; Part II., March, 1886.
1886. KEY, THOMAS,
Registration of Title to Land. 2 Law Quarterly
Review, July, 1886.
1886. MORRIS, R. BURNET,
Registration of Titles. [Prize Essay.] London,
1886.
1886. STEPHEN, SIR J. F.,
The Laws Relating to Land. National Review,
February, 1886.
1886. SWAN, JOHN,
An American View of the English Land Problem.
National Review, January, 1886.
1888. ANON.
Registration. Encyc. Brit., XX., p. 342, 9th ed.
1889. COUNCIL OF THE INCORPORATED LAW SOCIETY OF
LONDON,
Observations on the Land Transfer Bill. London,
1889.

NEW ZEALAND.

1878. OFFICE OF REGISTER GENERAL OF LAND,
Handy Book of the Land Transfer Acts (Torrens
System) containing Copies of Acts. By Author-
ity. Wellington, 1878.

UNITED STATES.

1898. ANON.
A Double System of Land Titles. Nation, Vol. 67,
No. 1725, p. 46, July 21, 1898.

## ILLINOIS.

1894. YEAKLE, M. M.,

The Torrens System of Registration and Transfer of the Title to Real Estate. 8vo, pp. xx, 255. The Torrens Press, Chicago, 1894.

## MASSACHUSETTS.

1891. ANON.

Suggestions upon some Points relating to Registration of Title to Land. Pamphlet, 8vo, pp. 10. Boston, 1891. (A very interesting and helpful discussion. Written by John L. Thorndike, Esquire, of the Suffolk Bar.)

1891. CHAPLIN, HEMAN W.,

Land Transfer Reform. Suggestions as to the Questions of Constitutionality. Harv. Law Rev., IV., p. 280, January, 1891.

1891. HASSAM, JOHN T.,

Land Transfer Reform: The Australian System. Harv. Law Rev., IV., p. 271, January, 1891. And Pamphlet, 8vo, pp. 22, Wright and Potter Printing Co., 18 Post Office Square. Boston, 1891. (In favor of Australian system.)

1891. RUSSELL, GOVERNOR WILLIAM E.,

Governor's Message, 1891. House, No. 49. (Commendatory.)

1893. BALCH, FRANCIS V.,

Land Transfer: A Different Point of View. Harv. Law Rev., VI., p. 410, March, 1893. (Practical difficulties.)

1893. BEALE, JOSEPH H.,

Registration of Title to Land. Harv. Law Rev. VI., p. 369, February, 1893. (Exposition and commendation.)

1893. CARRET, JAMES R.,

Land Transfer: A Reply to Criticism of the Torrens System. Harv. Law Rev., VII., p. 24, April, 1893.

1893. CHAPLIN, HEMAN W.,
    Record Title to Land. Harv. Law Rev., VI., p.
    302, January, 1893. (Need of Reform. Sug-
    gestions from statutes for "quieting title."
    Constitutional requirements.)
1898. CHAPLIN, H. W.,
    The Element of Chance in Land Title, Part I.
    Harv. Law Rev., XII., No. 1, p. 3, 1898. (La-
    tent defects of title not discovered by present
    system of Examination Reform.)
1898. MACKAY, H. W. B.,
    Registration of Title to Real Estate. Harv. Law
    Rev., XI., p. 301, January, 1898. (Historical
    and logical status, possibilities and difficulties of
    the system.)


NEW YORK.

1887. COMMITTEE OF NEW YORK BAR ASSOCIATION ON
    LAND TRANSFER REFORM. Majority Report.
    Martin B. Brown, Park Place, N. Y. Pamphlet,
    8vo, pp. 12. (In favor of the "Lot System.")
1887. COMMITTEE OF NEW YORK BAR ASSOCIATION ON
    LAND TRANSFER REFORM. Minority Report.
    Martin B. Brown, Park Place, N. Y. Pamphlet,
    8vo, pp. 15. (In favor of the "Block System"
    and the "Olmstead Bill.")
1887. OLMSTEAD, DWIGHT H.,
    Land Transfer Reform, or the Free Transfer of
    Land. Pamphlet, 8vo, pp. 116. Baker, Voor-
    his, & Co., 66 Nassau Street, New York, 1887.
    (Advocating "Torrens" and "Block" systems.)
1890 (?). COMMISSION OF LAND TRANSFER, Majority Bills
    of, No. 1.
    Pamphlet, 8vo, pp. 25. New York, 1890 (?).
    (Providing a Land Register Index on the
    "Block" system.)

# INDEX.

[References are to Sections.]

CERTIFICATE OF TITLE — *continued.*
> surrender of, to be conclusive authority to register instruments, 62.
> to be cancelled on discharge, 62.

*Original,*
> as conclusive evidence, 47.
> certified copies of, as conclusive evidence, 47.
> fee for entry of, $3, 110.
> first registered, how entitled, 42.
> memorandum on, of mortgagee's duplicate, 61.
> takes effect from date of transcription of decree, 42.
> to be cancelled on conveyance in fee, 57.
> to be noted how on conveyance in fee, 57.

*Owner's Duplicate,*
> as conclusive evidence, 47.
> cancelled on foreclosure of mortgage, 63.
> court of equity may order memorandum on, 85.
> court of equity may order cancellation of, 85.
> in case of tenants in common, 43.
> issued to owners in severalty, 86.
> loss of, notice of, given to assistant recorder, 55.
> memorandum on, of interest less than fee simple, 52.
> new certificate issued only on surrender of, 107.
> new certificate issued without surrender of, when, 107.
> new, issued on reversion after taking by eminent domain, 91.
> new, issued to grantor for unconveyed portion, 58.
> new, issued to grantee upon conveyance in fee, 57.
> new, issued to heirs or devisees of owner, how, 92.
> new, issued to purchaser under license of Probate Court, how, 93.
> new, to grantee of part, valid without certificate to grantor, 58.
> new, to heirs or devisees, memoranda on, cancelled after settlement, 92.
> new, to heirs or devisees, memoranda on, before settlement, 92.
> new, to include all land transferred, 58.
> nullification of, when surrender not enforceable, 107.
> one, covering several parcels may be exchanged for several, 44.
> petition for, when wrongfully refused, 107.
> presented with instrument, conclusive authority to register, 55.
> production of, may be ordered by court, 72.
> several, may be exchanged for one covering several parcels, 44.
> to be made by whom and how, 41.
> to be presented with mortgage deed, 61.
> to be surrendered and cancelled upon a conveyance in fee, 57.
> to contain memorandum of attachment, lien, or adverse claim, 72.

# INDEX.

**CERTIFICATE OF TITLE** — *continued.*
to whom to be delivered, 41.
where land lies in more than one district, 41.
*Subsequent to Original,*
how entitled, 42.
*Trustee's Duplicate,*
how issued, 65.
new, issued on surrender of former, 67.

**CERTIFIED COPY,**
fee for, of decree or registered instrument, 110.
of decree confirming mortgage sale, 63.
of decree for partition in relation to mortgage or lease, 87.
of instruments may be obtained, 56.
of mortgage or lease to be filed with application, 27.
of original certificates as conclusive evidence, 47.
of trust instrument may be registered, 65.

**CITATION,**
to bear test of judge and seal of court, 5.

**CLAIMANTS,**
under former owner bound by new certificate when, 55.

**CLAIMS,**
against estate, liability of heirs or devisees for, 92.

**CLAIMS, ADVERSE,**
arising after original registration,
affidavit of, how registered, 106.
frivolous, may incur double costs, 106.
invalid, registration of, to be cancelled, 106.
statement of, 106.
validity of, how determined, 106.
certificates of title free from all, — exceptions, 39.
fee for registering, $3, 110.
memorandum of certificate of, 78.
registered at time of transfer to be noted on certificate, 59.

**COMMISSIONERS,**
copy of return of, in partition proceedings, to be registered, 86.
deed of, when land sold by order of court, 86.
return of, in partition proceedings, as affecting mortgage or lease, 87.

**COMMONWEALTH,**
may have owner's certificate cancelled when, 83.
person absent from, may have trustee appointed when, 85.
to be subrogated to rights of plaintiff, when, 100.

## 90 INDEX.

**CONTRACT,**
action of, continued pending action of tort, 96.
action of, survives to representative of owner, 103.
action of, to be against whom as defendant, 97.
action of, to commence within six years, — exceptions, 103.
for damage or deprivation of land, lies when, 96.
other remedies to be exhausted before suing in, 96.
proceeds of action of, treated as real estate, 103.

**CONVEYANCE,**
memoranda of common forms of, to be adopted, 49.
when certificates granted subject to, without note, 39.
*Deed of,*
if registered, to be notice to all persons, 51.
operates only as contract and authority to register, 50.
to be executed by owner conveying in fee, 57.
to be filed and indorsed on conveyance in fee, 57.
*In Fee,*
how effected, 57.
of portion of land, how effected, 58.

**CORPORATION,**
application for registration by, 19.

**COSTS,**
may be borne by applicant, 36.
of survey, 36.
taxed as in Superior Court in Equity, 18.

**COURT OF EQUITY,**
decree of, may be registered like judgment at law, 85.
may order cancellation of certificates or entry of memorandum, 85.
may order execution of instruments to give effect to decree, 85.

**COURT OF REGISTRATION,**
a court of record, 2.
appeal from, to Superior Court, 14.
assistant judge of, 3.
assistant recorder to refer doubtful point to, 53.
cannot open original decree of registration when, 108.
clerk of, recorder to be, 7.
decision of, to stand if not appealed in thirty days, 16.
judge of, 3.
jurisdiction of, 2.
may be held by single judge, 4.
may cancel certificate in informations under Pub. Sts., ch. 182, 83.
may cancel memorandum on certificate of judgment in partition, 86.

94     INDEX.

DUPLICATE,
See CERTIFICATE, duplicate.

EASEMENTS,
unregistered, appurtenant to registered land, shall remain, 39.
unregistered, cut off by registration of servient estate, 39.

EJECTMENT,
judgment for plaintiff in, under Pub. Sts. ch. 175, for terms
less than seven years, not entitled to registration, 82.

EMINENT DOMAIN, 90, 91.
description of land or interest taken by, to be registered, 90.
lien upon land taken by, to appear in memorandum, 90.
memoranda of interest taken by, to be made on certificates, 90.
on reversion after taking by, certificate issues to reversioner, 91.
registration fees to be paid by authority taking by, 90.

ENCUMBRANCES,
certificate free from all, except what, 39.
certificate issued subject to, without note, when, 39.
discharge or release of, fee for registration of $.50, 110.
judgment in writ of dower registered as, when, 84.
memorandum of, on certificate, 78.
registered at time of transfer to be noted on certificate, 59.

ENTRY,
certificate of, on foreclosure, shall be registered within thirty
days, 63.
for possession, fee for registration of memorandum of, $.50,
110.

EQUITY,
court of, may order essential instruments executed, 85.
decree in, affecting land, registered like judgment at law, 85.
decree in, good if registered in sixty days when notice of
pendency has been given, 80.
proceeding in, not to affect land unless memorandum is
registered, 80.

ERROR,
remedy of one deprived of interest in land by, 96.

ESTATES,
less than fee simple, how registered, 52.
making up fee simple, all owners of, may get duplicate certificates, 48.
making up fee simple, names of all owners of, noted on all
certificates, 48.
of fee simple; see FEE SIMPLE.

# INDEX.

96 INDEX.

FEES — *continued.*

for entering decree of registration and sending memorandum. $1, 110.

entering order dismissing application for registration and sending memorandum, $1, 110.

entering original certificate and issue of one duplicate, $3, 110.

examining title, $5, and $\frac{1}{10}$ of 1% of value of land, 110.

filing and registration of adverse claim, $3, 110.

filing petition after original registration, $1, 110.

filing plan, $.75, 110.

indexing deeds recorded pending application for registration, $.25, 110.

issue of each additional duplicate certificate, $.50, 110.

making and entering new certificate and issue of one duplicate, $1, 110.

memorandum on mortgage, lease, etc., $1, 110.

note in entry, or registration book, $.25, 110.

notice by mail, $.25 and cost of printing, 110.

notice by publication, $.25, and cost of publication, 110.

registering attachments same as for recording, 74.

registration of certificate or receipt for payment of taxes, $.50, 110.

registration of discharge or release of encumbrance, $.50, 110.

registration of every instrument, $1.50, 110.

registration of levy or attachment or discharge of same, $.50, 110.

registration of mechanic's liens for labor, etc., $.50, 110.

registration of memorandum certificate or deposition of entry, $.50, 110.

registration of notice of issue of warrant in insolvency, $.25, 110.

registration of suggestion of death, $.25, 110.

service by sheriff, unchanged, 110.

of public officers, in cases not expressly provided for, 110.

FORECLOSURE OF MORTGAGE,

by entry and possession, 63.

may be impeached, 63.

may be made as of unregistered land, 63.

mortgagee may petition for entry of certificate after, 63.

on, by entry, certificate must be filed in thirty days, 63.

purchaser under, may obtain certificate, 63.

under power of sale under decree of court, 63.

under Pub. Sts. ch. 181, 63.

98      INDEX.

[References are to Sections.]

INNOCENT PURCHASER FOR VALUE,
holds free from encumbrances, when, 39.
interest acquired by, cuts off right of review in case of fraud, 38.
new certificate binds claimants under former owner in favor of, 55.
rights of, not to be impaired by court, when, 108.
rights of, saved from remedies for vendor's fraud, 55.
INSANITY,
of party to decree, court may appoint trustee, 85.
INSOLVENCY, 88–89.
assignee in, may get certificates of debtor's land, 88.
copy of decree vacating proceedings in, to be registered, 89.
copy of discharge from, with reconveyance, to be registered, 89.
messenger in, to register notice of warrant, 88.
notice of warrant against owner in, to be registered, 88.
notice of warrant in, fee for registration of, $.25, 110.
right by assignee in, to recover land, 70.


JOINDER OF PARTIES, 23.
JUDGE OF COURT OF REGISTRATION,
assistant, salary of, 13.
salary of, 13.
JUDGMENT,
affecting part of land described in certificate, 82.
against treasurer and others, execution against latter, 98.
certificate of entry of, for plaintiff, filed before registration of, 82.
copy of, in partition proceedings, to be registered, 86.
fee for registration of notice of, $.50, 110.
for defendant entitled to registration, 81.
for plaintiff entitled to registration when, 82.
for plaintiff in writ of waste registered as encumbrance, 84.
in action of ejectment not entitled to registration, 82.
in action under Pub. Sts. ch. 175 (terms less than seven years), not to be registered, 82.
in partition proceedings in relation to mortgage or lease, 87.
in partition proceedings to be entered on certificate, 86.
in writ of dower under Pub. Sts. ch. 175, registered as encumbrances, 84.
may be issued against treasurer alone when, 98.
may be registered within sixty days when, 80.
not to affect registered land when, 80.
on mortgage note not to affect title when, 63.

## 100 INDEX.

[REFERENCES ARE TO SECTIONS.]

LAND — *continued.*
    sold or set off on execution, 78.
    sold under lien for labor or materials, 78.
    sold under lien of mortgagee, or for payment of taxes, 78.
    taken by eminent domain.  (See EMINENT DOMAIN.)
    when divided into lots, plan to be filed, 44.
LAND REGISTRATION OFFICE, 8.
LARCENY,
    certificates shall be subjects of, 111.
LEASE,
    fee for memorandum on $1, 110.
    for less than seven years, judgment under, 82.
    for less than seven years to bind land, 50.
    for seven years or more authorizes registration, 50.
    for seven years or more not effective as a conveyance, 50.
    for seven years or more to be registered, 64.
    for terms under seven years, certificates granted subject to,
        without note, 39, ¶ 4.
    form of, no change in, 50.
    when registered prior to partition proceedings, 87.
LEGAL INCIDENTS OF REGISTERED LAND, 70.
LEGAL PROCESS,
    service of, upon non-residents, 22.
LESSEE,
    certificate of, to be registered after partition proceedings, 87.
LESSOR,
    tenant of, to register lease after partition proceedings, 87.
LETTERS OF ATTORNEY.
    See ATTORNEY.
LIABILITY,
    for betterments, etc., when certificate granted subject to,
        without note, 39, ¶ 5.
    of heirs or devisees for claims against estate, 92.
LICENSE,
    to deal with land, jurisdiction of Probate Court to grant execu-
        tors, administrators, and guardians, not impaired, 93.
LIEN,
    affecting land to be registered in district where land lies, 71.
    affecting portion of land, to describe portion, 71.
    for labor and materials, 77.
    for labor and materials, fee for registration of, 110.
    if registered, filed, or entered, to be notice to all persons, 51.
    liability of land to, 70.
    may be continued, or discharged, 73.
    mechanic's, fee for registration of, 110.

## 102 INDEX.

# 106 INDEX.

**RECORDER** — *continued.*
shall attest alteration in registration book, 108.
  be clerk of court, 7.
  be sworn, 11.
  be under direction of court, 8.
  have custody of documents, 8.
  keep accounts of fees, 11.
  keep indexes of decrees and applications, 49.
  mail notice of application, 32.
  make no memorandum on certificate unless owner's duplicate be presented, 55.
  not alter registration book, 108.
  not enter certificate if owner's duplicate not presented, 107.
  notify Attorney-General of application when, 32.
  notify mayor or selectmen of application, when, 32.
  pay assurance fund over to Treasurer, 95.
  pay receipts quarterly to Treasurer, 11.
  prepare indexes and entry books, 49.
  publish notice of application, 31.
  report case to register of deeds, 29.
  send certified copy of decree to assistant recorder,
term of service, 7.
vacancy in office of, 10.
**REDEMPTION,**
  after expiration of time for, court may grant entry of new certificate, 79.
**REGISTERED LAND,** 29.
**REGISTER OF DEEDS,**
  authority of, 10.
  to be assistant recorder, 10.
**REGISTRATION,**
  an agreement running with the land for continued registration, 45.
  application for, of title, who may make, 19.
  assurance fund to be paid on original, 94.
  court may order, after default, 35.
  decree of. See DECREE OF REGISTRATION.
  effect of, when procured by fraud, 55.
  fee for filing petition after original $1, 110.
  judgment for plaintiff entitled to registration, 82.
  of adverse claim, fee for, $3, 110.
  of cancellation of interest less than fee simple, 52.
  of certificate or receipt for payment of taxes, fee for, $.50, 110.
  of decree affecting or quieting title, 85.

# INDEX. 107

## 108    INDEX.

110 INDEX.

[REFERENCES ARE TO SECTIONS.]

WASTE,

judgment for plaintiff in writ of, to be registered as encumbrance, 84.

WAYS,

laid out under Pub. Sts. ch. 49, § 65, certificates granted subject to and without note, 39.

WILL,

of owner, certified copy to be filed on application for new certificate, 92.

probate of, when memorandum not required in, 80.

to take effect as conveyance of land, 50.

WITHOUT PREJUDICE.

See PREJUDICE.

WRIT OF ENTRY,

not to affect land when, 80.

officer serving execution in, to register attested copy within three months, 83.

WRIT OF ERROR,

not to affect land when, 80.

www.ingramcontent.com/pod-product-compliance
Lightning Source LLC
Chambersburg PA
CBHW030616270326
41927CB00007B/1198